Working the Present,

Mindfully-Based

Bringing Mindfulness-Based
Group Work Into
Individual Therapy

Written by
Donald Fleck, LCSW, MBA
Diplomate in Clinical Social Work

Illustrations by
Liz Kresch
Artist & Yoga Teacher

Working the Present, *Mindfully-Based*

Bringing Mindfulness-Based Group Work Into Individual Therapy

Published by
Donald Fleck
280 Park Avenue South, Suite 17L
New York, NY 10010
917-202-5148
www.learnmindfulnessnyc.com

Print Version Cover and Interior Design
Robert Lanphear
www.LanphearDesign.com

Ebook Cover and Illustrations
Liz Kresch
www.BreathAndBones.com

Fleck, Donald.
Working the Present, Mindfully-based: Bringing Mindfulness-Based Group Work Into Individual Therapy/Donald Fleck.

ISBN: 978-0-9967300-1-3

1. Psychology

ENDORSEMENT BY

Zindel V. Segal, Ph.D.

In *Working the Present, Mindfully-Based,* Donald Fleck succeeds in staying true to the intentions of MBCT while adapting it for use in individual therapy. The book can be used with clients who have serious mindfulness meditation practices as well as those just getting started, as Fleck has taken many of the core elements of MBCT—the 3-Minute Breathing Space, Kindness and Self-Compassion, Working with Difficulty, Allowing/Letting Be, Thoughts are not Facts, Kindness in Action—and found ways to use them effectively within the basic dyadic encounter.

Packed with clinical vignettes and a user friendly narrative structure, *Working the Present, Mindfully Based,* provides a clear path towards offering this novel delivery format for MBCT's key concepts and practices.

—Zindel V. Segal, Ph.D.,
Author of *Mindfulness-Based Cognitive Therapy for Depression*

Why this Book

Mindfulness-Based therapies are getting a lot of attention these days, to say the least, and they are very effective in a group format. But clients meeting one-on-one expect sessions geared to their unique needs. They expect therapy to be about their progress or difficulty in working towards their unique treatment goals. In the eight years I have been teaching Mindfulness-Based Cognitive Therapy I have tried taking my individual clients through the content only to be reminded again and again that the weekly discussion of progress and difficulties takes priority over a curriculum.

So, over the years I have sought out new ways to use the powerful elements of Mindfulness-Based therapies within the individual session. With the approach in this book, therapists can continue with the methods they find effective, and add in mindfulness elements as needed.

For example, if a client comes in very upset about an interaction with her colleague, we might start with our normal therapy process, inquiring into what happened before and after, how intense it was, how she understands it, how she tried to work with it, how it relates to her childhood and parents, and how it relates to homework and treatment goals and her recent work in therapy. Then we might introduce a mindfulness practice. We might bring her experience into the present, asking about her experience right now, in thoughts, feelings and body sensations. We might ask her to bring to mind again the interaction with her colleague, let it sit in her awareness, noticing the feelings that arise as she does this. We might ask her to allow those feelings to be present, to de-couple them from thoughts and instead link the feelings to sensations in her body. In this way she may build tolerance for these feelings. As she is more able to tolerate them, she will be more able to think clearly and take actions that are helpful to her. We might ask if she could practice this Working with Difficulty process at home, so we can discuss it more next week. We might wrap up by returning to our usual way of working, perhaps relating this experience to her patterns and interactions with other important people in her life.

Overview

A detailed table of contents is available after the Introduction.

Introduction

Practicing mindfulness means bringing mindfulness into our own life, using mindfulness in our work with clients, and helping our clients use mindfulness to work with difficulties.

Mindfulness of pain and the healing process

Bringing mindfulness into our own life can be like a trip to the our favorite vacation spot, but one that doesn't end because we can be mindful anywhere, anytime. When we are awake to the sounds of birds as we walk to work, to the feelings of our bodies as we sit in our chair, to the taste of our dessert as we eat it, life can take on a lighter hue and our spirits can lift. When we are in session wondering why the client isn't getting better as fast as we wish, we can use the mindfulness-orientation to remember that the client's next right action may well be the one that sets her on a new helpful course.

But there's a downside to mindfulness, at least for the beginner. While mindfulness can be like a trip to our favorite vacation spot, it also can be like a trip to a smelly garbage dump. Here's why:

> If we are aware of our experience in the present, there's no possibility of editing out the bad stuff. We will encounter what we like and, inevitably, what we don't like.

Without mindfulness we may be able to avoid unpleasantness, things like smelly garbage, unhappy memories, scary thoughts, movies that upset us, information that is painful. For example, I once gave a friend a subscription to The National Geographic. He found the articles on global warming, the preservation of species, the environment, too upsetting. So he asked me not to renew the subscription after a year. He didn't do anything wrong; he was just not yet ready to tolerate the level of upset caused by the articles.

Encountering what we don't like may be a downer for some. Who wants more contact with the unpleasant underside of life? I don't, but I have to. Living a life with blinders on has a huge cost. The blinders may eliminate much of both the wonderful and the awful. By putting on blinders to what we want to avoid we impoverish our life, unless we live on Tahiti. Actually, even Tahiti has mud. On the other hand, without the blinders we can experience both the wonderful and the awful; we just need a new set of tools to help us tolerate the awful.

Why don't we hear this about mindfulness, that it includes awareness of smelly garbage and other things we prefer to avoid? Because all those folks actively avoiding the garbage are not looking for a journey that runs by a dump.

Fortunately there is a way to work with this. We teach mindfulness with non-judgment, by which we mean acceptance. We smell the garbage, we accept it. It is here, we might as well know it. We haven't gone looking for it. It is simply here. This idea of acceptance is in the moment. We are not accepting that we will always smell garbage, we don't have to park the car in the dump. We just need to experience it in this moment. That is not so difficult an experience, when it's just for now.

···

Definition: Mindfulness is awareness of present experience: the good, the bad and the neutral, with acceptance.

···

With acceptance, without judgment, the experience is different: we realize our experience is impermanent, transitory, ever changing, even interesting. When we are not using up energy avoiding garbage dumps we can use our energy to fuel our curiosity, our interests, things that fascinate us.

For example, if I am on my way home from a formal event, all dressed up, and walk up the stairs from the subway, see water on the steps, realize it is raining, then realize I have no umbrella with me and I am about to get soaked, I might start fuming. My best clothing, soon to be soaked. Most people at this point might curse the weather, themselves, or both, and walk home, getting soaked, with a heavy, angry heart.

With mindfulness there is another way. I am aware I will get soaked. I am aware I can do nothing about it right now except to allow it to happen. I accept this. After all, there is nothing to be done. I just walk out into the rain. At my normal pace. Rushing would not reduce the soak. I feel the raindrops on my face, feel my clothing getting heavier, feel my socks getting wet with cold rain. Curious, I turn my face upwards, better to feel this cold water. I allow myself to experience this 'getting soaked'. The frustration leaves me. What's to be frustrated about? I'm soaked.

It works the same way for things we enjoy. If we are eating our favorite dessert, something we have been looking forward to all meal, we may find ourselves talking with our friend or partner about what we will do later that evening, not even tasting the dessert after the first bite. With mindfulness we develop a practice of allowing the taste of the dessert to be present in our awareness, savoring every aspect of it. We learn many ways to enjoy our dessert, engaging our 5 senses, perhaps even noticing our feelings as we eat it. In the same way many otherwise ordinary experiences can really come to life.

Moving beyond acceptance of the unpleasant, we can add in a sense of patience to this experience, allowing the experience to be around during its natural course. Allowing doesn't mean we grasp at it, but that we simply let it take its course. So, we smell the garbage, and it persists until the wind blows in the other direction, or until our walk or our drive takes us somewhere else. For the person caught in the rain, there is no need to stand in the rain until it passes, but just to walk home.

This allowing is like gradual exposure. We learn tolerance of unpleasantness. The next time we encounter it, we are less upset because our tolerance has increased.

With the calm that comes from mindful awareness, then allowing and acceptance, we may find our mind has cleared. We are no longer flooded with worry, or a need to get away. With a calm mind, we are able to see possibilities that eluded us when we were trying to avoid things. We are better able to choose wise, helpful actions that can better our situation.

Let's say I'm on my way to a difficult meeting. I'm worried I'll be met by hostility. In my mind I am busy running through different scenarios. In my mind I try out confronting the hostility. I try out being conciliatory. I try out arriving with my mouth open. I try out listening carefully. The thoughts churn on and on. I hear a bird, as I'm walking to the meeting, I see a tree. I've become aware of the present, I've become mindful. I check in with myself, making note of my thoughts: getting racy. My feelings: worried, angry. My body: shoulders tense. I realize I've been trying to control the outcome of the meeting. I realize I can't control it, I accept that. I allow the worried, angry feelings to remain, I give them space. This allowing could be scary, but I've practiced it many times. I know that feelings keep evolving, they often don't stay the same. I know that by allowing them to remain I become less afraid of them. I realize I must simply be alert in the meeting, I accept that I cannot control it. After a short time my mind clears. Wise actions become apparent: I need to listen carefully, speak my truth.

This is a process of mindfulness that can be very helpful. It grows out of that need to be mindful of the garbage as well as the roses. What we first saw as the rub, the dirty underside of mindfulness, becomes the rub of the magic lantern that releases the Genie of calm, clear mind.

The process is short:

1. **Aware** – We increase our awareness of the present. When we are present, we perceive more, we perceive differently. When our clients are aware, they have stepped out of automatic pilot.

2. **Allow** – When we practice allowing our experience to continue, without chasing after it, or running away from it, we find we have more strength to work with it. Same thing for our clients.

3. **Accept** – When we accept our experience as it is, just for now, or go a step further and accept ourselves, our energy can move from resistance to relief and finding solutions. Same for our clients.

4. **Act** – When ready, we act. Our actions propel us forward in life. Getting the next action right is really important. This is how change starts. This is how change continues. With awareness, allowing, and acceptance we are grounded and better able to choose helpful actions. Clients, too.

So, read on, and you will learn ways to build this process into your own life, into your sessions with clients, and into your clients' lives.

Let's Take This Journey Together

Learning mindfulness is a process and a collaborative effort. Even as I offer my understandings to you, still I have the mind of a beginner, experiencing once again each element I describe, deepening my understanding as I write this. I encourage you to do the same, perhaps reading the material several times. So I write with the "we" in order to include myself and the reader.

Use Caution, Please

Every effort has been made to clearly explain mindfulness in psychotherapy. However, a manual cannot substitute for supervision or individual instruction. It is your responsibility to use prudence with these practices.

There are risks. For example, people with a history of trauma that hasn't been processed can experience strong feelings. Mindfulness may be very helpful for these people, but it will need to be applied within a safe relationship and with an understanding of ways to let the material come in gradually.

Case examples – Details have been changed to protect the privacy of all concerned. In most cases these are condensed or composite interactions.

Link to Audio Tracks
for Use with this Manual

Readers are welcome to use the set of audio tracks recorded by the author for use in facilitating Mindfulness-Based Cognitive Therapy (MBCT) groups in New York City. They are stored in the internet cloud, in a service called Dropbox. Buying this book gives the right to work with these tracks for yourself and your clients. Readers are welcome to download the files to their computer or other device, but not to sell or give them away.

The link to audio files, and the Mindful Events Calendar, is at the end of this book.

Table of Contents

CHAPTER ONE
Quick Start Guide

I have several shelves of books on mindfulness, many of them on mindful psychology. I really enjoyed reading them. I especially value the ones that tell me actual practices I can use, and when they might be helpful. I want to do the same for you. So here are a dozen valuable practices. I use all of them.

The one I use most often is #12, The Pause. This is a way of simply stopping and noticing what is present. I might notice something internal, like my thoughts, my feelings, or my body, or I might notice something external through my senses.

Just now I took a pause, and felt my mood lighten, as my thinking took a break. I had been buried in editing this manual. My thoughts were very focused. Pausing, I also became aware of an anxious feeling, and some tightness in my throat. I saw details of my office, a picture, a color on a wall, I heard the air conditioner. I heard voices outside. After the pause I felt connected to the world outside my head. I had become present.

We don't have to go to grad school to begin using mindfulness with our clients. We don't even have to read this manual first. This chapter outlines a dozen practices we can begin using right away. However, if we feel that we don't have enough background in this, by all means we should read the manual and find a guide who has practiced mindfully with clients. And read the paragraph "Use caution, please."

If we're ready to start now, we first work with one of the practices ourselves, so we can become familiar with the experience of it. We try it multiple times when we have different moods, until we have a feel for the range of experiences that might occur.

Then we can try introducing it to some friends, so we can develop ease in describing it and leading someone through it. If we have some friends who already understand the benefits of mindfulness and others who are resistant, some who are therapists and some who are not, we can then practice introducing the practice to a wide range of people. If needed, there are scripts in the manual for us to adapt. Once we have done this for one practice the others will come more easily.

1. Basic Awareness of Breath
This can be useful at the beginning of a session.

In our own meditation we may have found that just a few breaths help center us. Once we have experienced this for ourselves it is just a small step to bring it to others. All we need is a brief introduction, something like, "I find that if I take a few breaths I often feel centered and more present. This may prove helpful for you also. Would you like to try it?" If our client is receptive we might sit together for a minute or two, depending on what feels comfortable. We might give some basic guidance, such as, "Let's try closing our eyes, if that's comfortable, and form an intention to notice our in-breaths and our out-breaths. When our minds wander into thinking, it's not a problem, we simply return to noticing our in-breaths and our out-breaths."

2. The 4-Right Nows
For beginners to tune in to the present, anytime

We notice contact with our chair. We notice our body, the contact with our clothes, the pressure of our feet on the ground, whatever comes to our attention. We notice our breath, on purpose, with curiosity about the shape of each breath. We notice sounds, be they loud or soft.... we bring curiosity to noticing these sounds. We do all this as slowly as we wish. The steps:

1. We notice contact with our chair

2. We notice our body
3. We notice our breath
4. We notice sounds

3. Mindfulness of everyday activities with CBS

When it's hard to do something with awareness.

CBS stands for Curiosity, Breath awareness, and Slowing down. If we decide to take a shower mindfully, we bring curiosity to the process (what body sensations do we notice, fro example?). We bring in awareness of our breath, and we slow down just enough to get ourselves out of automatic pilot.

If we decide mindfully to stand up, we bring curiosity to how our body shifts to do this, what muscles are used, what the body feels like. We notice our breathing as we do it. We do it slowly. If we are fast, we get lost in habit energy. When we slow down, it can feel like doing it for the first time. When doing a mindful activity we use:

1. Curiosity
2. Breath awareness
3. Slowness

4. Walking Mindfully

A mindful meditation we can do just about anywhere.

Walking is one activity we don't have to slow down to do mindfully. All we need to do is intend to stop thinking. We do this by noticing the movement of our feet, along with our breathing. As we do this we may notice the things we are passing as we walk. We may notice sounds, children perhaps, or beeping horns, or birds. We take it all in. The benefit is that we are practicing mindfulness while we are doing something we have to do anyway. We learn right away that when the mind stops, there are lots of interesting things to notice. The steps:

1. We intend to walk mindfully
2. We notice the movement of our feet and our breathing
3. When the mind takes over we return to awareness of our feet and breath… judging is not required!
4. If we need more help focusing on our walking then we can add in another awareness, in addition to walking and breathing. We can bring in awareness of sounds, or of the air on our face. Or we can fill the mind with a little saying, such as, "Left foot, right foot" as we walk.

5. Mindful Breathing

A way to feel breathing as a physically grounded act.

We often find ourselves lost in thought. Clients find this. Therapists find this, too. When this thinking is not needed, or not wanted, or is actually harmful, we can anchor ourselves in the present, allowing the thinking to take a little rest. We do this by bringing into awareness our breathing. We set an intention to notice the full length of each in-breath, and the full length of each out-breath. (See the instructions for practice #1). We follow our breath as a physical event, feeling it in our body. Many of us find it most helpful to notice the slight expansion of our belly as we breathe in, and the slight falling away as we breathe out. When thoughts come in we return our attention to our breathing, with kindness for this very human, wandering mind. The steps:

1. Notice our breathing
2. When we realize we've been thinking, returning our attention to our breath

6. Noticing Our Body

The most basic training for mindfulness,
getting to know our body.

We want to have more awareness of our body, since so much of our life is known through body sensations. At first we take this on faith. After some practice we realize that our body is a rich source of information. We start anywhere. This time we start by noticing our feet: contact between the toes, warmth or cold, wetness or dryness, then the rest of our feet. We bring this curiosity to the rest of our body: Noticing our legs, then our hips/groin, then the back of our torso, then the front, then our hands/arms, then our neck, then our head. We then can practice holding our whole body in awareness, and watching how different parts of our body draw our attention moment by moment.

7. Mindfulness of Feelings

A way to work with feelings.

When feelings are getting strong enough that we feel a want to attend to them, we can stop what we are dong, and focus our attention onto them. We may feel an urge to divert our attention, to distract ourselves so that they will go away. This is a natural inclination, any many people do this for all their lives. That is the way of aversion, a way of avoiding. The trouble is, at best we are diverted but the feelings are still there. At worst they increase in strength. So here we try out a different way. We put our attention onto the feelings. We let the thoughts take a break. We consciously bring our attention right into the feelings. And we notice what is happening in our body at the same time that the upsetting feelings are present. Perhaps a tightness in the chest or belly, perhaps something in the throat or face. The process goes like this:

1. We notice we are upset, that feelings are here
2. We let go of our thinking, perhaps by following our breath
3. We bring our attention towards the feelings, not away from them
4. We intend to keep our attention on our feelings and on our body

Note: When attention is on feelings and thoughts, they may fuel each other. When attention is on feelings and the body this helps to ground us, helps to let the feelings just be, and at some point to flow through. If at anytime the feelings move towards overwhelming, going back to our usual methods, or distracting ourselves.

Each step offers help. When we slow down, we send a signal to the brain that things are not out of control.

When we recognize this as a long-term pattern we might realize we do not have to find a solution right now.

8. Mindfulness of Thoughts

A way to work with thoughts.

When thoughts are becoming insistent, rushed, perhaps with an obsessive quality, we can get lost in them. Then again, we get lost in just about any thoughts: shopping lists, even. So the first step when we realize this is happening is to take a few breaths with awareness, and to consciously slow down whatever we are doing. We can take a pause, or do the 4-Right Nows, or follow our breath, for example. Then we can take a look at the thoughts. Are these thoughts part of a frequent pattern of worry or rumination? Are they patterns of thinking we have had many times before? As these thoughts swim around in our head they can be hard to get a grip on, so we try writing them down; sometimes, when we do that, they are seen more objectively, because now they are specific. Do these thoughts carry emotional content that I am avoiding? What happens if I let those feelings into my awareness and sit with them? The process, then, goes like this:

1. We become aware that our thoughts right now are a problem for us
2. We take a few breaths with awareness
2. We slow down our activity
3. We examine the thoughts
4. Do they carry feelings that I am avoiding?
    (If so, trying #7 Mindfulness of Feelings)

9. Three-Way Check-in

A great way to tune-in to internal experience through thoughts, feelings and body sensations.

Note: this is the first part of the powerful 3-Minute Breathing Space.

We notice what thoughts are in our mind.... We notice what feelings are present.... We notice any discomfort in our body, or whatever in our body comes to our attention. This is the 3-Way Check-in. It is a way of becoming centered in the present. Ideally we do it several times a day. This helps us develop a habit of mindfulness. The steps:

1. What thoughts are in our mind?
2. What feelings are present, however small?
3. What discomfort is there in our body, or what comes to our attention in our body?

We then return to the activities of our day

10. Noticing Pleasure

Using the 3-Way Check-in to become more aware of positive experience.

Forming an intention to notice good things, we go about our day with the intention that, when something pleasant happens, we will really notice it, in detail. So, when we feel pleasure, we do the 3-Way Check-in. We notice what thoughts are present. We notice what feelings we are having. We notice what happens in our body as the pleasant thing is happening. And we write it all down. We make this a practice. We allow ourselves to have whatever thoughts, feelings, and body sensations are there, we accept that these are the pleasures of the moment, and we keep going, perhaps with a little smile. The steps:

1. We set an intention to notice pleasant things as they are happening, several times a day

2. We notice our thoughts, feelings, and body sensations
   (3-Way Check-in), when we notice something pleasant
3. We accept these as our experience in the moment
4. We keep going, perhaps with a smile. Why seek joy when
   pleasure is so readily available??

Note: Write your observations on the Mindful Events Calendar

11. Sitting with Body Discomfort
A basic practice of working with physical difficulty.

When we stub our toe, our instinct is to make the pain go away as
quickly as possible. With mindfulness we try to practice noticing
the pain, then allowing it to stay with us for a bit before we rush to
action. This 'allowing' may bring acceptance, and a response rather
than a reaction.

The steps:

1. We become aware of the pain
2. We allow it to continue in awareness for a little while,
   perhaps accepting that it really is painful, right now
3. We realize some wise action we can take

12. The Pause
A simple stopping in place,
leaving ourselves open to noticing experience.

We set an intention to let thinking pause for now. Then we notice
anything that comes to our attention in the present, perhaps
sounds, perhaps something we see, perhaps some body sensation,
perhaps some feeling. When we pause and notice the present,
we may discover something interesting: our experience of this
moment.

CHAPTER TWO

The Mindfulness Orientation

Walking down the street I am thinking about what I want to write today. Some worries about today's clients pop in. I remember a difficult session from yesterday. I feel anxious and a little sad. I hear a bird singing, and when I hear it a small miracle occurs. I wake up to the present. The thoughts stop. I feel my mood lighten: I am simply walking to my office, it's enough just to be aware. Lost in thought I was in a sort of automatic pilot, the thoughts influencing my mood and even my body. Awake to the present I pay attention to my senses, now I notice other people, and I smile. I see the sky and I smile. I feel my body. Thank you bird!

Mindfulness is a way of working in the present that can help us and our clients know life directly rather than through a veil of thoughts. It could be called present-focused work.

It offers ways to intensify sessions with moment-by-moment awareness, to enlighten our clients around some sources of their difficulties, and ways to lighten their burdens through various mindfulness practices.

The central focus of much psychotherapy is talking. It has been called the talking cure, or talk therapy. We will continue to use talk as a central part of psychotherapy. The mindfulness orientation just adds an interest in present experience. How is the present to be known? Much of this manual answers that question. For now, it may be helpful to note that becoming interested in the present often means adding awareness to two different areas of experience. First, noticing internal experience, known through thoughts, feelings and body sensations. Second, noticing external experience, known through sight, sound, touch, taste and smell.

Mind-wandering Happens to the Best of Us

This transition from knowing things mostly through thoughts to knowing things through mindfulness won't tend to happen unless we first become aware of just how prominent thinking is. One exercise for the uninitiated is to set the intention to stop all thoughts for just one minute. Looking at a timer, watching the seconds tick by without any thought coming into our mind. We can try this, and many of us will find the results interesting. It is a rare person who can empty their mind this way.

Another exercise is just to keep one particular thought out of mind. Let thinking go on as normal, but just make sure this one word does not enter our awareness for a minute. Let's try it with the word, "giraffe." How did we do? It is a rare person who can keep a given word out of awareness, also So, we realize it will take some work to quiet the mind enough to become mindful. Much of the work of meditation is learning to calm the mind. But meditation is not our emphasis here. It is not a necessary skill for mindfulness as applied in mental health.

Instead, we can use the mind that won't be controlled as part of the therapy process. Learning mindfulness is a lot about accepting what we encounter. Accepting our thinking, for example, rather than trying to change it.

Present-focused Therapy

Present-focused sessions play out quite differently than in traditional talk therapy. For example, Mary might report in session that she had a disappointing date. We might help her recollect details. Perhaps there were some intense, difficult moments. We know how to work with these already. With mindfulness we can also ask how she is feeling moment-by-moment as she is recalling this. If intense in the moment, we can teach her how to stay with these feelings, how to investigate them, and we can help her build tolerance for them before they become overwhelming.

If we have taught Mary a few mindfulness practices, she can use them outside the session. She might use them on her next date to get a deeper understanding of that person and her reactions, by noticing her internal moment-by-moment experience in addition to her normal thinking processes. She might use tools that allow her to stay with her emotions rather than trying to avoid them, so that she can gain understanding of her flow of emotions. She would certainly have a richer, deeper report to make in the next session.

In a way mindfulness is about working with the experience of the client as they are sitting with us. This may feel new. Perhaps we are used to finding out how the week went, and using that as a starting point for our session. Then we might explore our client's experience, and work together to find ways to do things a bit differently in the week to come. This is working in the past and the future.

Or we may really help the client go back to her early years and re-frame her understanding of her past, and re-experience some of her feelings as a way of healing and moving forward. This is working in the past.

Or we may focus on some anxiety-provoking event that is coming up, perhaps a wedding, a career change, a date, or a performance. This is working in the future.

That can be effective psychotherapy. I do it all the time, and we are not going to abandon it. We are just going to add in another dimension.

We Start With Ourselves

Working in the present will feel pointless until we begin to inhabit the present a bit more for ourselves. We eat some dessert. We start by realizing that while eating we may find ourselves forgetting to enjoy it, instead talking about past desserts.

We begin by realizing how emotionally rewarding it is to live in thoughts of the past and future. We may find the present boring if we focus on it for very long. Thinking about the past and the future offers a chance to anticipate wonderful times beyond the boring experience of the present.

Focusing on the present does not have the quick pay-off of imagined happiness when we focus on the past or future. To value the present we need to learn a whole new way of experiencing the present. Ways to enrich it.

But what choice do we have? Living in the past and future offers a sort of imagined life, in which we rarely come down to earth to smell the roses and the dirt from which they grow. When will the time be ripe enough, rich enough, that we can happily just settle into it? Seemingly, not very often. The ease that comes from living in our minds, in the past and future, can be intoxicating.

In the process of learning to know the present we find a world of experience that our stressful lives and our habits of thinking have closed off from us.

In the process of learning and working with mindfulness we enrich our lives. We help our clients enrich theirs. And most importantly, we find a whole new bag of tools to help clients move forward with their lives.

We are well trained in working with the past, and in using the client's early childhood, formative experiences, and current life to help the client understand herself, and to bring up and resolve feelings from the past.

We are well trained in working with the future. We understand that unconscious fear of death influences much, and that anxiety about the future can be worked with productively in session.

We are practiced in living in the past and the future in our own lives. In discovering and learning the practice of mindfulness within psychotherapy we are learning to experience and investigate the present.

And when else but in the present can life be enjoyed?
If not now, when?

So…. How about we pause for a moment right now, with the 4-Right Nows?

• MINDFULNESS EXERCISE •

Reading these instructions then intending to become present, right now:

Closing our eyes.

Right now, feeling our contact with our seat, as a way to become present.

Right now, noticing our body.

Right now, becoming aware of our in-breaths and our out-breaths, feeling them in our belly as an anchor to the present

And right now, listening to sounds, as a way to connect to the present.

Allowing ourselves to slow down for a few minutes as we just sit here, with these experiences.

And when we're done, opening our eyes, and returning to the activities of our day.

. . . .

We need to experience and to have a regular practice of mindfulness. The biggest obstacle is getting over the harsh self-criticism that "I'm not doing it right," and making it a happy habit so that we say to ourselves, "When will I practice today?"

To help establish the habit we can join an existing weekly group of meditators, or begin our own, recruiting a like-minded colleague. To find an existing group, try searching the internet for "Meditation group - my town" or "sangha - my town."

If we already have an established mindfulness meditation practice we might consider modifying it to the type of practice most helpful to psychotherapy clients, who generally will have the harsh self-critical voice telling them "You can't do this right," who may give up new activities easily and who might have a habit of avoiding unpleasant moments. The practices in this manual are geared for people who are self-critical, who don't need another experience of failure.

Self-disclosure of Our In-the-moment Experience

In classical Freudian psychotherapy we consider the therapist to be a blank slate that the client can project his stories onto. There is no self-disclosure. Currently, many of us disclose some things about ourselves, some times. We know that the disclosure must not be for our needs. If we self-disclose it must be for the good of the client.

With mindfulness we realize another form of self-disclosure. We consider sharing how we are experiencing our present moments with the client. For example, we might share how we are feeling as the client tells us of a struggle, or what we notice in our body. The guideline is the same: will it benefit the client if we self-disclose? Sometimes our disclosure helps the client know how others respond to them. Sometimes it helps the client have a corrective "parental" experience. Sometimes it encourages the client to mirror our disclosure. All we need is to be aware of our experience in the present (perhaps via a 3-Way Check-in) and to have some understanding of whether disclosure might be helpful.

Learning Experientially

We learn from ourselves that much of mindfulness is best learned through direct experience.

Thus, part of the process will be giving ourselves home practice assignments, and doing the same for our clients.

Working with clients who tend to have low self-esteem, we will quickly realize when they are setting their learning goals too high. This may happen often. The cost of this will be discouragement as they fail to meet their goals. So it is very important that the goals are not set too high.

Half-goals

We ask clients how much they would like to practice in the coming week. Whatever they pick, we worry that the goal is too high. So we cut it in half, asking them if that would be enough to make the effort significant. If they agree, we cut it in half again, and ask again. We continue in this way until we get to the minimum goal that they agree would be a significant effort. In this way we reduce the probability of disappointment and reinforcement of negative self-perception.

For example, say we have been talking about mindfulness and paying attention to just one thing, and how when we try to do several things at once we send a signal to our nervous system that things are not ok, that we need to rush to survive. Our client has an idea: she will not multi-task for a full day, and see if that leaves her less wired. Interesting idea, we say. Would it be enough to intend to single-task for half a day? Two hours? One hour? A half-hour? We keep going until our client has reduced the goal as much as possible, but still feels it would be a significant effort.

Buddhism

Buddhism is the source of much of the wisdom used in practicing mindfulness. Buddhism offers a coherent system developed over several thousand years. Many do not consider Buddhism to be a religion. But some clients will feel it is, and resist religious influence.

We can help all our clients by taking a secular approach so that we do not come up against their beliefs, so that our work is acceptable to all of them.

Practicing mindfulness is so new that many of the current great teachers are themselves Buddhists, and refer to Buddhist teachings regularly. We need to be very grateful for these teachers. Their lectures and texts teach and inspire us. In this work, however, we are secular even as we respect and learn from the Buddhist sources.

We follow the tradition of Jon Kabat-Zinn who secularized Buddhism when he created Mindfulness-Based Stress Reduction for use in medical settings.

Mindfulness + Acceptance = Hope

Perhaps we start with clients by identifying a problem and figuring out a way we can help them get better.

With mindfulness we can add another possibility: that we can help clients accept themselves as they are. Ironically, with acceptance change can come more easily.

A client may come to us believing he is defective, that he needs to change before he can feel better. He may believe that something is wrong with him, that he has failed a life. With that mindset he may feel hopeless.

When we teach him acceptance of his current condition, when he can say "This is my experience right now, this is me right now," without a compulsive need to change, then he may well experience a sense of calm within himself in that moment, and with that calm an improved ability to get some perspective on his situation, and with that he may see some new choices, some new actions he might take, and this might give him a new sense of possibility.

This acceptance does not mean a willingness to stay with bad situations, but rather a moment-by-moment warm-heartedness towards herself in the now, a realization that despite everything she is alive, breathing, and in that there is hope that her next actions may be wise and helpful.

In this sense practicing mindfulness is a kind of movement toward wholeness, a sense that we can accept the present and also plan actions that will be helpful.

Not Emotional Regulation

Introducing mindfulness is not a practice of emotional regulation. In emotional regulation we learn to feel less intensely; for example, we learn to stop anger from arising before it becomes overwhelming and leads to actions we regret.

What we do practice with mindfulness is building emotional tolerance. With stronger emotional tolerance we are able to

experience a feeling intensely without becoming overwhelmed.
For example, we might feel the full force of the anger, and still not
act on it.

Sometimes emotional regulation is exactly what is needed. A
person has a problem punching people, we help solve the problem
by teaching ways to keep the feeling from getting so intense. In
emotional regulation we seek to change the person, so they stop
the feeling.

At other times, emotional tolerance is exactly what is needed. In
building emotional tolerance we work with the person as we find
them. We teach the person to feel the feelings, to let them flow
through. We teach the person to accept the feeling, in the sense that
we know it is there and do not try to push it away. Then the person
may notice that choices come to mind, that there are alternatives to
physical escalation. In this sense we are not saying the person has to
change, but rather that we can help them change how they relate
to their experience and find that they have more choices than they
realized. This may be true for anxiety, sadness, OCD, panic, social
anxiety or many other situations of concern. We can learn to accept
and to find that we have more choices than we realized.

CASE EXAMPLE:
Integrating Mindfulness into a Full Session

*Joan comes in for depression and anxiety. Joan's sadness relates to
a decline in her work income, her ill-health, and a tendency toward
isolation. Her anxiety revolves around financial insecurity and she
is easily upset by this and a wide variety of other issues. We have
completed a piece of work around her sadness and are now working
on her anxiety. The session begins...*

Therapist: Here we are.

Joan: Yes.

Therapist: How about we start with a few minutes of
breathing meditation?

Joan: OK

Therapist: (I sound the bell, close my eyes. I check, Joan has also closed her eyes. We have done this many times before. She is familiar with this practice. No need for instruction.)

Therapist: (During the 5 minutes my head clears, my mind slows, I hear some birds outside my window, a feeling of happiness arises in me. The change in me is profound I feel more accepting of myself. A memory comes in: 2 weeks ago Joan asked for a hug at the end of the session. We had hugged, the therapist's version, with limited physical contact. Last week Joan had explained she wanted to thank me, with that hug, for my work with her. Now I wondered if she was having some discomfort with that intimacy. It had been a surprising moment for me. Oh my! Perhaps my intimacy issues had interfered with my own tuning-in for this session.)

Therapist: (I sound the bell to signal the end of this meditation period.)

Joan: Don, I am feeling really low. It seems like nothing is working for me. I don't have enough money coming in, I'm worried my skills aren't as good as they were, and I don's see any way out. I met with my stock broker this week and he says I need to invest more aggressively. He explained some investments, but I don't understand them. I don't know what to do.

Therapist: And is that how you feel right now? And how is it in your body?

Joan: Right now I am feeling really stupid. My stomach is tight. I don't feel there's any way out.

Therapist: (I have the choice of asking Joan to sit with these feelings or explore some links. I opt for the second.)

Therapist: Hmmm.... I'm remembering how you felt when your Dad died. You were 17. You were the oldest child of 4. You were told that you had to manage the home because your Mom had to get a job.

Joan: Wow, yes I remember. This is something that goes way back for me.

We take some time to explore that. Joan remembers how unfair it felt having been given adult challenges, and felt sad right now, as she remembered.

Therapist: Can you sit with that feeling of sadness, let it ride, stay with it for a bit here?

Joan: Sure. (She had done this before. She closes her eyes, uncrosses her legs, sets both feet on the floor, and is silent.)

Therapist: (After about a minute) How is it for you right now?

Joan: I'm OK, I'm really feeling sad.

Therapist: And what are you noticing in your body?

When feelings intensify, we can ask the client to focus on the feelings and the body at the same time. This does not chase the feelings away, but helps keep them from escalating, as can happen when awareness is on thoughts and feelings.

Joan: I feel some tightness here, in my chest, and my stomach hurts a little.

Therapist: (After letting Joan sit with those feelings awhile.)

We continue the session with an exploration of her situation.

CHAPTER THREE

Aware: We Work in the Present

Caught at a big dinner table my mind begins going down a familiar road of negative self-judgment, I feel boring. I feel pressure in my head. I sit there. I am trapped in automatic pilot, the thoughts and feelings are totally real to me. Then I realize I've been drinking a lot of water, I need to pee. In the bathroom I see myself in the mirror. I become aware of myself. I become aware of the present. I take a deep breath. Sadness becomes clear to me at that moment, and I just keep breathing, letting it ride. I realize I must return to the table. But now it will be different. I am aware of the full intensity of my feelings. I will let them be in me until they pass. I have an increased interest in what my friends are saying. At some point, I enter the conversation, feeling part of it all again.

With mindfulness we practice noticing the present. But why? Isn't the present sort of boring? The raisin exercise is a dramatic way to introduce present-awareness. It helps us understand how much of our experience we are missing by living in our heads, on automatic pilot.

Find a raisin and a place to sit quietly. Then work with the text below. We might take some breaths after each sentence, as a way to slow down and deepen this experience. For some of us this will mean 2 breaths between sentences, for others 5.

Instructions: Eating a Raisin Mindfully

1. Take a raisin and hold it in the palm of your hand, look at it, taking your time. Examine it, get to know its details. What is the overall shape? What shapes are on the surface? What

colors do you see? Try turning it over and examining what you see on the other side. What do you feel when you touch the raisin? What do you notice if you squeeze it between your fingers? Try bringing it up close to your ear, and rolling it between your fingers…do you hear anything? Bringing it to your nose, do you notice smells?

2. Think about bringing the raisin to your mouth. Slowly bring the raisin close to your lips, but not touching, noticing how your arm knows exactly how to do this. Bring the raisin back and forth a few times, getting to know how your arm moves. Touch the raisin to your lips, and pause with it there, noticing what it is like when the raisin touches your lips. Open your mouth and slowly place the raisin inside, but do not chew it. Let it sit on your tongue, without chewing it, just letting it sit there. Noticing the contact of the raisin with your tongue. Moving it so it rests between your teeth, noticing how your tongue knows how to move it. Let the raisin sit there a bit. Close your teeth on the raisin, taking one bite, and stop to notice what happens in your mouth. Take another bite. Chew slowly. As best you can, don't swallow the raisin, as it breaks into small pieces. This may be hard, no one's perfect. Then prepare to swallow, noticing how your tongue positions the raisin in your mouth.

3. Swallow the raisin, noticing movements in your mouth and throat as you do this. Perhaps even feeling the raisin going down your throat. Noticing your mouth after this.

4. Now let's examine your experience. Let's start with your sensory experience – sight, touch, sound, smell, taste. What did you notice with your senses…What was your direct sensory experience? Let's hold thoughts about it for a moment. (For example: I saw brown, purple, ridges, it smelled sweet, etc.)

5. Ok, now let's think about how this is different from the way we usually eat. How was this different? (For example: It's slow, it's focused, I really tasted it, it was rich, etc.)

6. Now let's think about why this might matter, this way of directly experiencing. (You might have noticed, for example: I miss out on so much, there's a lot to appreciate that I just don't notice, I always thought raisins were ordinary.)

We can learn so much from that simple raisin. But there's more.

There is another way to experience the present. The first way is externally, through the 5 senses, as we did with the raisin. The other way is internally, through noticing our body sensations, our feelings, and our thoughts.

Body sensations = anything we feel on or in our body
Feelings = emotions, broadly defined
Thoughts = words, images, memories, ideas, concepts

We introduce this by noticing pleasant things.

Pleasant Events

We help our clients by asking them to be alert for something happening that is nice, pleasing, pleasant. We ask that they deepen their awareness of the experience, using principles of mindfulness. We work with the Mindful Events Calendar.

• MINDFULNESS EXERCISE •

Practice using the Mindful Events Calendar, focusing on pleasant events. Try to notice them as they are happening. **Note:** the Mindful Events Calendar can be used to mindfully observe things that are pleasant or unpleasant. We start with things that are pleasant.

Mindful Events Calendar

A place to record—and look into—events that moved you. They may have been pleasant, unpleasant, or confusing.

Some people use this for a few weeks, as a practice of noticing thoughts, feelings and body sensations. Others make it a regular practice.

Suggestion: make copies of this chart and carry it with you and write down the things that you are noticing.

MONDAY	TUESDAY	WEDNESDAY	THURSDAY	FRIDAY
What happened?	What thoughts were present?	What emotions were present?	What body sensations were present?	What do you notice as you write this?

MONDAY	TUESDAY	WEDNESDAY	THURSDAY	FRIDAY
What happened?	What thoughts were present?	What emotions were present?	What body sensations were present?	What do you notice as you write this?
Example: I saw a squirrel in the park, it was eating a nut.	*"What a nice sight. How easy it is for that squirrel. It's just enjoying what it has."*	*Happiness, content-ment.*	*A warm sensation in my chest, a lightness in my step after I moved on.*	*There's pleasure in noticing nature.*

This noticing things that are pleasant, on purpose, can be a real eye-opener. All we are doing is having the intention to notice nice things, then to enrich that experience in the present by noticing how it affects us, internally. Some of us decide we want to do this daily, as a general practice of awareness.

Once people have some experience noticing things they like, we can ask them to notice things then don't. This is part of a general progression in learning mindfulness, where we start with the popular preconception that mindfulness is about happiness, and gradually help people move towards mindfulness of all experience, which can be curative and balancing.

CASE EXAMPLE:
Moving towards the unpleasant

Jessica was afraid she'd have to urinate, and this fear was keeping her from traveling around the city to appointments. Often the urge came on so strong she had to step into restaurants to use the bathroom. She feared that one day she would not find a place to urinate. She was so troubled by this fear she considered wearing a diaper. Her doctor gave her medication to repress the urge, but it had side-effects she could not tolerate. We tried some behavioral interventions, to no avail. One day we discussed the possibility of her bending forward in her chair, putting pressure on her bladder, as a way to moving towards the feared sensations rather than trying to avoid them. This of course got her to feel the urge even more intensely than before. She did this hesitantly and reported that the sensations were tolerable, did not produce fears that she would wet herself at that moment.

The next week I asked her to repeat this leaning forward to increase the pressure. This time Jessica reported that the urge to urinate kept decreasing as she held the pose. Interestingly, her other fears also had diminished from last week to this. In the third week we discussed the idea of moving towards unpleasant experience, how that changes our relationship to the experience, in her case removing the fear and even some of the sensations of having to urinate.

Practice Focusing our Attention

Noticing our experience in the present, externally or internally, isn't too hard but we find that our attention wanders. We need a way to train our attention, and that way is called meditation.

So we practice keeping our attention on one thing. The breath is a popular choice, but we could focus on anything. We practice this meditation daily for 10, 20, 30, 45 minutes. We set for ourselves a length of time that works for us. There is no magic number that is "enough." We start with the guided meditation tracks on Dropbox, even if we have experience, so we can practice working with thoughts in this mindfulness-meditation approach.

It is easy to assume that learning to focus means that the less our mind wanders the better we are doing. This is not true. With traditional meditation that is the goal, but with mindfulness meditation the goal is to stay present, but only as much as our mind with its present energy allows. We practice acceptance of this wandering mind. We do not strive to have it produce less thoughts. We work with what we have.

— MINDFULNESS EXERCISE —

Practice using the 10-Minute Breath Meditation audio track. Or use the text below.

Script: 10-Minute Mindfulness of the Breath

1. This will be a 10-minute mindfulness meditation on the breath. Let's start by becoming mindful of our seat, feeling the contact with our chair... Placing both feet on the ground. Finding a place where our hands can be still... Noticing the shape of our spine, adjusting it so that we can breathe easily, and have a sense of pride in our posture... Allowing our eyes to close, if that's comfortable... If it's not, then just soft focusing our eyes on the floor a few feet in front of us... We want to minimize visual distractions while we sit....

2. Becoming aware of sounds...Sounds are a great way to bring our awareness into the present, to become mindful of the present... Noticing the big, obvious sounds, as well as the smaller ones...

3. And now intending to notice our breathing... Noticing the full length of each in-breath, and the full length of each out-breath... Perhaps noticing the movement of our belly as we breathe... The belly slightly rising on the in-breath, slightly falling away on the out-breath... We practice making the breath a really physical experience, noticing the physical movement in our belly... We use the word intending to notice our breath because we know the mind can wander away from our desired focus of attention.

   We say intending instead of making a promise to ourselves, or a vow....

Our intention here is just to notice the breath as it is. We are not trying to change it in any way. No need for the breath to be deeper. No need for it to be longer. No need for it to be regular. Just noticing the breath that we have.

4. When we notice that our mind has wandered, we just return to noticing our breathing....

5. We may find that we are disappointed at how much our mind has wandered. Perhaps it is wandering most of the time. Perhaps just a little. Either way, we may wish it wandered less. So, we become interested in how we relate to ourselves when we realize our mind has wandered, that we've been thinking.... We may find that we are self-critical.....Yet what happened is normal, this is what minds do! So we see how much self-acceptance we can muster, normalizing this wandering mind. We try out embracing this mind that thinks, we see with how much acceptance we can bring to awareness of our breathing. Maybe even giving ourselves a little smile, since a good thing just happened: we remembered we were intending to focus on our breath.

6. So... where is our mind right now? If thinking, we see how much acceptance we can bring to that, and simply return to our breathing.

7. Just noticing the full length of each in-breath and each out-breath.... Noticing it in the movement of our belly, rising and falling....

8. Intending to notice the breathing. Noticing our mind has wandered.... recognizing that as a happy moment. Good going....

9. Now, getting ready to end this mindfulness meditation on our breathing. Noticing sounds..... Noticing our contact with the chair...... then taking one or two more breaths with awareness, and opening our eyes and looking around. And returning to the activities of our day.

Positive Self-regard
and Learning Mindfulness

The first thing we notice when intending to meditate is that our attention does not stay on the breath. We've assumed we had pretty good control over our minds, we went to school, got some good grades, learned how to fill our minds with information and understanding, but until mindfulness came along we never really tried to give our mind a rest, to empty it. The emphasis was always on filling it up. We may never have tried to stop and just notice one thing.

So, many people realize for the first time that their mind wanders. For some it wanders only a little, for many it wanders quite a lot. We are aware that people already are very self-critical, so we refine our practice in a way that does not make this worse. We tell ourselves we intend to focus our attention, we don't vow it. This lets in awareness that this is a practice, not a perfection. In addition, we work with those moments when we discover our attention has been wandering. It is all too easy to feel we have failed if we were meditating for 10 minutes and 8 of them were filled with thoughts. We normalize this. We practice accepting this with thoughts like, "This is just how my mind works, I'm doing the best I can, it's OK"

In practice, we are learning self-compassion along with learning meditation. Some research indicates that this learning of self-compassion is itself a critical part of mindfulness when learned in a mental health setting. Also, many have found that when self-compassion is nurtured, so also is compassion for others. When compassion for others is nurtured, self-compassion also comes more easily. It is as if there were a compassion button in us, and it is either on or off.

Now if I asked you to memorize the date of the signing of the Magna Carta, and you forgot...how would you feel? For myself, I'd be somewhat embarrassed, but would easily admit my forgetfulness and move on. But if I asked you to concentrate on your breath and you could not... Well, if you were me awhile ago you might think, "Why can't I do this easy thing? What's wrong with me? Am I just now discovering that something is seriously wrong with my mind?" and then, I'd think, "I'd better not tell anyone until I've practiced and learned to control this crazy mind."

When learning mindfulness we encounter aspects of ourselves that we never knew before, like this wild mind. That puts us right smack in front of our tendency to hide out when we encounter something really awful about ourselves. This tendency to hide out, often related to low self-esteem, is a willingness quickly to believe that we are faulty. It has been well explored. It is the basis for the Alice Miller book, *The Drama of The Gifted Child*, in which she wrote about so many children feeling shamed for being their true selves, and learning to hide themselves, and to present a 'false self' to the world; quite a tragedy.

For many of us, this tendency to deny the naturalness of our own experience is the water we swim in. This is such a norm that we are not even aware of it... it's just part of our background experience. It's so easy to think, "There I go again, messing up...." But after some practice it can become easy to think, "Ahhh, here I am being me again!" This is a very nice development, because we are accepting ourselves as we are in that moment.

The tendency to judge ourselves harshly may suffuse many aspects of our experience. For example, sometimes we might notice ourselves about to speak in a group but then find ourselves holding back because we think maybe what we have to say would not go over well. We might worry that people think we're overly sensitive. We might worry that we're taking time away that would allow someone else to speak. Or we might worry that we really are stupid and that by opening our mouth we will allow other people to see this terrible flaw in us.

We learn to face up to that in order to learn mindfulness. Mindfulness is about becoming aware of our experience as it happens, with acceptance.

In learning mindfulness we must deal with this low self-esteem, and its opposite, Positive Self Regard. I've coined this term from Carl Rogers' name for the accepting therapist having Unconditional Positive Regard for her or his patients. The idea is that we learn to water the seeds of Positive Self Regard in ourselves, and when we water them, nurture them, we strengthen them.

When we're learning mindfulness meditation this becomes really important because in order to talk about our experience of mindfulness meditation, we need to speak about what's really going on inside us. And it's very easy to feel that we're doing it wrong. It's very easy to feel that our active mind shouldn't be so active. It's very easy to feel that emotions that come up in us are somehow wrong. It's very easy to feel that meditation is just for other people. However, these are the very things we need to able to speak about in order to learn our meditation. Every time we practice acknowledging these feelings internally and with people we trust we are watering the seeds of Positive Self Regard.

So it's really helpful to think about the idea of Positive Self Regard.

I'm not talking about the power of positive thinking in which we might say "I'm the smartest person on earth, I'm going to get this job no matter what." Because that's more in the realm of fantasy, and it's future oriented. We're really talking about noticing aspects of ourselves that might seem negative or neutral and realizing them as phenomena of right now, not necessarily permanent, noticing them with acceptance, and in the context of our whole selves. And then practicing saying them out loud, among friends or in therapy.

Interestingly, many have found that when positive self-regard is nurtured, so also is positive self-regard for others. When compassion for others is nurtured, self-compassion also comes more easily. It is as if there were a compassion button in us, and it is either on or off.

Simply put, when we realize our mind has wandered off, we return our attention to our breathing. But how we do that is really important. We have a choice at the moment of realizing to be self-critical, or self-congratulating (because we have just remembered what we intended to do.)

We Must Enjoy Meditating
...or Forget It

If we were teaching a baby to walk, we probably would encourage him by saying things like, "Good try...There you go...One more time... You're doing so well!" If we were a harsh teacher, and every time he fell we said, "bad boy," the baby would soon lose interest in practicing.

We may have a hard time identifying with such a harsh teacher, yet we may unconsciously be exactly that teacher with ourselves.

When we are learning to meditate we tend to criticize ourselves when our minds wander. With thoughts like these we will not keep learning meditation for long. We will give it up.

Instead we can develop the voice of the loving parent teaching the baby to walk. We tell ourselves, "this is normal," "this is expected," "this is just how my mind works," "this is me," I'm doing the best I can" or something like that. In short, we can be kind, gentle and loving to ourselves.

And if our mind is still wandering after eight days, or eight months, we can continue in this way. There are many bonus points for those of us who learn to be gentle with ourselves, to accept ourselves, as we are. We can even begin to see the moments we realize our mind has wandered as learning opportunities!

When we learn to be gentle, to bring joy to meditating, we will continue. Rewarded behavior tends to be repeated!

Exercise: Practice with the 20-Minute Seated Meditation. It includes meditation on the breath, the body, sounds, and thoughts. This is included in the Dropbox tracks.

We Can be Creative
with our Focus of Attention

There is an endless variety to the ways we can intend to focus our attention. Many choose the breath. When following our breathing, there is an endless variety of ways we can do that. We might concentrate on only the out-breaths, the moment at the end of each out-breath, the breath via the movement of our belly, the breath felt in our nostrils or our chest.

Or we can choose a different focus altogether. We can choose any of the senses, or feelings, or the body, or even thoughts themselves. Or we can chose an external object such as a photo. There is an endless variety, and we may find that each one is useful in a different way.

Compassion Can be
Learned Directly, Too

Through accepting the mind we have, we practice learning positive self-regard. We can also develop a positive view of ourselves in a direct manner, through a form of meditation called Loving-Kindness Meditation, sometimes shortened to LKM. (There are many variations. The one below is inspired by Barbara Frederickson, in her book *Love 2.0*.)

We Assess for Strengths Before We Use
Loving Kindness Meditation

Because self-criticism runs rampant in mental health, it can be difficult to look at ourselves with eyes of love. Embedded in the idea of Loving Kindness Meditation is the idea that we need to change somehow before we can feel happy, which can lead us to feel that once again we have failed. So, we are cautious when we introduce this practice.

Developing compassion for a benefactor can be a good place to start. Most of us can do that. We begin by choosing a person who has helped us, a relative, a friend, a teacher, a spiritual guide. We close our eyes and meditate awhile to become present. We bring to mind an image of that person's face, in a relaxed moment. We think of some things that person has done that have benefitted us. We hold them in mind. We then imagine that we are filling our hearts with as much loving-kindness for that person as we can, as well as with compassion and gratitude, and then we imagine we are transmitting that energy to our benefactor. After awhile we say silently to ourselves over and over these compassionate phrases, inserting the person's name or using he/she:

May _____ feel happy
May _____ feel safe
May _____ feel healthy
May _____ live with ease.

(We say "May she feel happy" rather than the traditional "May she be happy" because we are avoiding making this into magic, but rather just intending for a feeling state of acceptance.)

We continue until we feel we are finished. If we lose our initial enthusiasm, we bring to mind more positive things this person has done for us.

Sometime after this we go through the same process for a difficult person in our lives. This not should be a very, very difficult person, or at least not until we were very familiar with these practices. We just choose a person who has given you some minor upset, perhaps the waiter who knocked over our water glass. We do the practice just like the above, including thinking of some positive things this person has done for us or for others, filling our heart with as much kindness as we can muster for this difficult person, transmitting it, then using the compassionate phrases above.

Finally, we are ready to practice on ourselves. We save ourselves for last because, in this culture, we may be the hardest person to love. As above, thinking of several things we have done that we feel were helpful to ourselves or to others, and filling our heart with as much loving kindness as we can. But then imagining we are sending that loving kindness to ourselves, a sort of special gift. And then do the compassionate phrases above.

We can make this a regular part of our practice, experimenting with details in order to make it comfortable for the unique person we are.

Script:
Loving-Kindness Meditation (LKM)

Inspired by the work of Dr. Barbara Frederickson in her book Love 2.0

1. Let's start by becoming mindful of our seat, feeling the contact with our chair... Placing both feet on the ground. Finding a place where our hands can be still... Noticing the shape of our spine, adjusting it so that we can breathe easily, and have a sense of pride in our posture.

2. Allowing our eyes to close, if that's comfortable... If not, then just soft focusing our eyes on the floor a few feet in front of us... We want to minimize visual distractions while we sit....

3. Now... bringing to mind a person who has been a mentor, or a spiritual guide, or just someone who brings a smile to our face when we think of them.... it is ok if this person is alive or not. Imagining we can see their face, in a relaxed state, not in a formal photo, just their everyday face, holding it in our mind's eye...

4. Now thinking of several nice things they have done for us, or some way they have helped us, or some good qualities they have... and holding those in our awareness....

5. Now imagining that we are filling our hearts with feelings of love and kindness for that person... all the love and kindness we can muster in this moment, as we hold in mind the nice qualities or actions of this person....and adding in compassion for this person....

6. And then imagining that we are transmitting these feelings from our heart to that person's heart...

7. Now continuing to hold this person in awareness, And offering these thoughts to them. Just saying these phrases silently to ourselves as we think of the person. (I'll use the pronoun she)

May she feel safe
May she feel happy
May she feel healthy
May she feel at ease with her life

Repeating this process for a person who has been a bit difficult for us.

8. Now thinking of ourselves.

Choosing ourselves is a choice. We could choose a person who is neutral, a person who troubles us, or all people, for example.

Just imagining that we are looking at our face, in a relaxed everyday expression....

And bringing to mind several things we have done that we feel good about, or several positive qualities we feel we have....

Then filling our heart with as much love, kindness, gratitude and compassion as we can....

And then transmitting it from our heart to our self....

OK, great. Now continuing to hold ourselves in awareness, And offering these thoughts to ourselves. Just saying these phrases silently to ourself.

May I feel safe
May I feel happy
May I feel healthy
May I feel at ease with my life

9. And now reconnecting with our seat, noticing it. And noticing sounds. And then taking one or two more breaths and then opening our eyes and looking around.

Tuning-in to Mindfulness

We develop our mindfulness practice at the same time that we're developing our meditation. Mindfulness and meditation complement each other. By mindfulness we mean awareness of our present experience.

We start by choosing things to do mindfully. Here are a few examples:

Cleaning:
Brushing our teeth
Showering
Washing the dishes

Moving:
Walking
Standing up
Getting out of bed

Eating:
Sipping our coffee or tea
Eating dessert
Eating cold French fries

Note that the first 2 in each group are things many of us enjoy, and the third one is one many of us do not enjoy, that we find unpleasant. We can try working with a variety of mindful activities, learning different things from each one.

When we are learning mindfulness we can practice noticing externally (through the senses) and we can practice noticing internally (through thoughts, feelings and body sensations). We experiment and find ways of mindfulness that easily ground us in the present.

We begin by practicing with things we enjoy, learning to directly experience them, increasing our ability to savor them, to appreciate through direct experience. Then we try some that we don't enjoy.

We realize that forgetting mindfulness is easy, so we take steps to establish a habit. We may set an intention to do certain things mindfully each day. We may try linking mindful activities to already established habits such as eating a meal. In that case we may work on the habit of noticing the first bite of something at every meal, for example. As with meditation, we need to be mindful of the self-critical voice. So we may choose to notice the first bite, but still accept if we don't notice any bites til the last, so that we so we can nurture positive self-regard.

Or we may pause and notice sounds every time we walk to work.

Or we may mindfully notice the eyes of each person as we say "Hello," to them. We use our creativity to choose intentions, and we experiment with what works for us.

Working in the Present

We can apply these 3 core skills (mindfulness, meditation and compassion learned directly or indirectly via the LKM) in many ways. For the sake of simplifying our learning we can make a few of them very specific.

4-Right Nows

We get in the habit of noticing the 4-Right Nows,

1. noticing our contact with our chair
2. noticing our body
3. noticing our breath
4. noticing sounds

Any of these can bring us out of thinking and into awareness of the present, and together they are even more helpful. Noticing our chair we are reminded of how much we keep out of awareness, and how solid this awareness of the chair is, how grounding. Noticing our body we remember we are sentient beings. Noticing our breath we remember we are alive. Noticing sounds we are reminded that hearing can give us much pleasure, when we are aware of it. Noticing sounds we remember a world outside our jumble of thoughts.

Case Example:
Therapy enhanced by mindfulness

Pete had trouble controlling his sadness, at times he could barely get out of bed. He came to me hoping mindfulness would help.

We had a few sessions to give him some basic skills. He used the pleasant and unpleasant events calendars in order to practice bringing his attention into the present, and in order to learn the idea of the 3-Way Check-in. He used some brief guided meditations to focus on the present through his breathing. He began doing some activities, shaving and sipping his tea, to become mindful at different parts of the day. Two sessions back I noticed that he was practicing less, then not at all. So, at the end of the previous session I prescribed no mindfulness activities, suggesting he take a break from it, there were other things we could be working on.

Arriving for this session, he seemed calmer than usual. He was clean shaven, and well dressed. Often I had a sense he seemed distracted. We explored some material around his functioning, work issues. We had a really productive session. As he was about to leave, he remarked, "I decided to meditate before our session, did it for 9 minutes. It was pretty good. I did the 4-Right Nows, noticed my contact with my chair, noticed my body, noticed my breath, noticed sounds, and slowed myself down." So now I understood the source of the calm he had brought into this session.

Mindfulness can help in very general ways. In Pete's case, it helped him relax into the moment before his session. A person can begin to practice mindfulness, or to meditate, and go about their business with more awareness, less stress, more calm and more focused, even listen better. Pete reminded me of that. If Pete could achieve this by himself before session, imagine what he might do when guided by us during his sessions.

The 3-Way Check-In

At some point we might begin practicing the 3-Way Check-In, asking ourselves,

1. "What am I thinking right now?
2. What am I feeling?
3. What am I aware of in body sensations?"

Each time we do this we are taking a snapshot of ourselves, as we exist in that moment. We may learn some interesting things! If we perceive ourselves as depressed, we may find that at various times when we do this 3-Way Check-In, that at that moment we are happy, or neutral. If we perceive ourselves as always thinking about a person, we may find that at various times we are thinking of others. We may encounter a strong or interesting feeling. We might ask ourselves if we can let that feeling be in us, not trying to change it, but just to rest in the knowing of it. Having awareness of it, accepting it (in the sense of knowing its reality), allowing it, and even wondering if a right action comes to mind in response to it.

We might adapt this for clients, thinking of it as a kind of pause, when they are at an intense emotional moment in therapy. Or perhaps as they are telling a story without much feeling. Either way can be helpful. Perhaps we might say something as simple as, "Do you mind if we pause for a moment," or "How are you right now?" or "What are you noticing right now?" We might add, "Are you noticing any feelings, no matter how large or small, whether they make sense or not?" Or we may add, "Are you noticing anything in your body right now? Any areas of tightness, discomfort or holding?"

We are asking about their internal experience in the moment. We ask about feelings and body sensations. We do not need to ask about thoughts unless they have not been speaking.

At times when the feelings are intense, or are getting more intense than is helpful, we might ask our clients, "How does that feel in your body?" The principle here is that when we have a feeling connected to a thought the thought and feeling can feed on each other, each increasing the intensity of the other. Sometimes that is helpful. At other times we sense that the emotion or thoughts are getting so strong that they are creating a traumatic moment and we act to interrupt this self-reinforcing cycle. We do this by asking them to focus on the feelings and the body at that moment. Sometimes we direct them towards noticing the lower back, stomach, chest, shoulders, neck, eyes, mouth, face. Feelings felt in the body often do not have a reinforcing quality; they can remain as they are. We are not avoiding them, just not feeding them.

We can get in the habit of pausing, just stopping the thinking for a few moments, or a minute, and noticing our experience in the present. We can do this ourselves, and we can ask our clients to pause. Then we can return to the material or choose to ask the client to sit with the feelings, and take it from there.

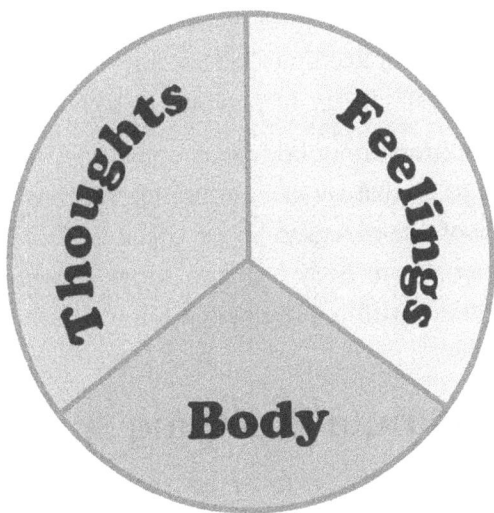

Illustration: 3-Way Check-In

We notice, "What thoughts are here right now, what feelings? What body sensations?" We can think of internal awareness of the present as encompassing these 3 elements: Thoughts (in which we may include images and concepts), feelings (meaning emotions, broadly defined), and body sensations (which may include sensations inside and on the surface of our bodies).

Noticing our thoughts can be helpful because immediately we have de-centered from them; when we look at them they are not us, they are thoughts of the moment. With some practice and exploration we may realize that there is a stable self that is aware of these thoughts.

Noticing our feelings can be helpful because we often are not aware of them. We notice the really strong ones, be they about a dessert we are really enjoying, or something that brings us to tears, but we may not be aware that feelings are present much of the time, just not strong enough to take over our awareness. So intentionally noticing feelings brings us in contact with a part of our selves we were not aware of. When we have feelings outside of awareness they may influence our actions in ways we don't realize. When we are more aware of our feelings, they can exert less control, or at least we realize what is controlling us. Also, checking in frequently on feelings helps us realize through direct experience that while feelings feel like they will last forever, often they are momentary, they can change surprisingly quickly.

And we check in with our body sensations. Our minds are such powerful parts of us, that we can go through much of life with awareness only of our thoughts. So we check in with our body sensations. After all, our body is us, too. Much of what we experience in the present, with mindfulness, is known through the body.

3-Minute Breathing Space

A more formal version of the pause and the 3-Way Check-in is also available, and was developed as a unique part of Mindfulness-Based Cognitive Therapy (MBCT). It is called the 3-Minute Breathing Space. It is useful for a regular check-in to current experience. And with a small modification it is useful when clients find they are beginning to spin out into overwhelming experience.

Briefly, the 3-Minute Breathing Space has 3 steps:

1. Doing the 3-Way Check-In to become aware of present experience.

2. Focusing this present awareness down to one point in our body, into the felt-sense of the movement of the belly as we breathe.

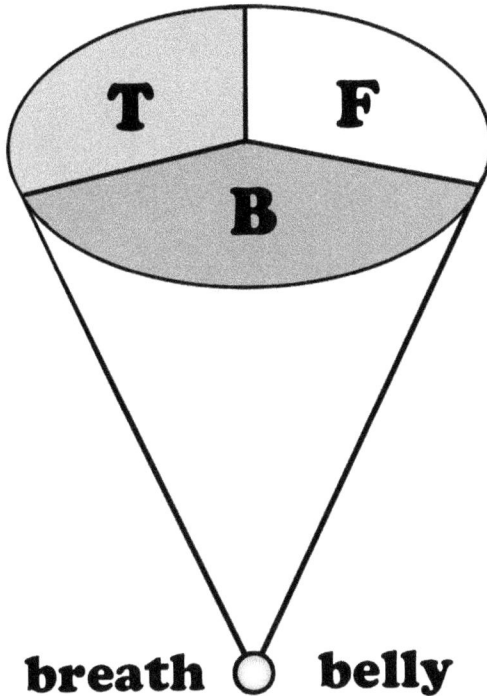

Illustration: First and second steps of the 3-Minute Breathing Space

First we do the 3-Way Check-In, then we focus our attention down to one place in our body, to the movement of the breath in our belly. Note: we use T for thoughts, F for feelings, and B for body.

3. Broadening this felt-sense from the belly to an awareness of the whole body. With this body awareness we are ready for re-entry into our "doing" life, the body-focus available to keep us aware of the present.

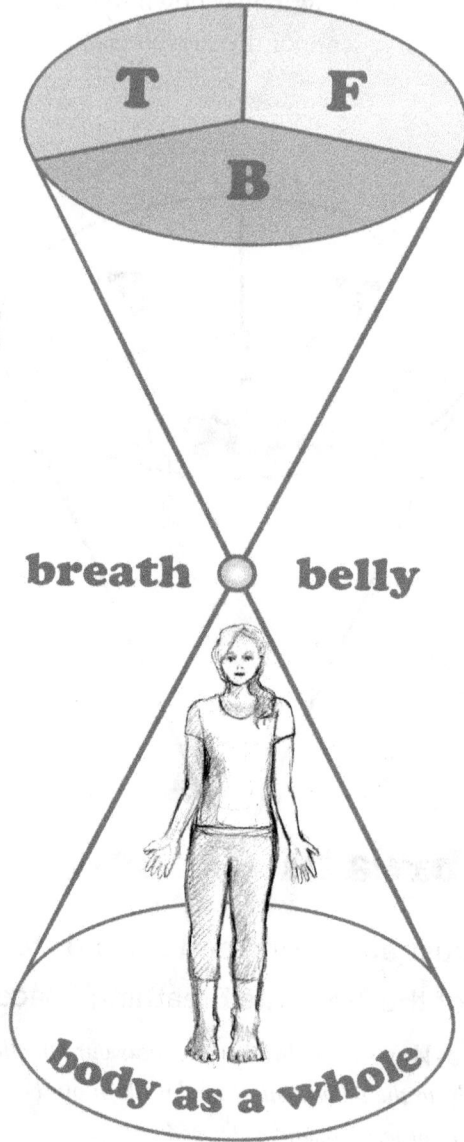

Illustration: The 3-Minute Breathing Space

Adding the third step, becoming aware of our whole body, and with that present-moment awareness feeling ready to return to the activities of our day. Note: we use T for thoughts, F for feelings, and B for body.

Exercise: Practice the 3-Minute Breathing Space. This is included in the Dropbox tracks.

Script: 3-Minute Breathing Space - Regular

First, drawing our attention to our experience in the present, doing a 3-Way Check-in: noticing our thoughts... noticing our feelings... and noticing whatever body sensations come into awareness... When we have done that, just letting in a thought, something like, "Ah.... so that's how it is for me right now, these thoughts, these feelings, and these things I noticed in my body." So, now we are aware of our present experience, our thoughts, feelings, and body sensations.

Second, focusing this awareness of the present down to one particular point in our body, by bringing our attention to the movement of our breath in our belly. The slight expansion of our belly on the in-breath, and the slight falling away on the out-breath.

Third, expanding this awareness of the breath in our belly out to an awareness of our whole body. We may scan around our body as we do this, or it may be easy to hold our whole body in awareness.

And then returning to the activities of our day.

Note: The intention here is not to change ourselves or our experience in any way. It is to bring our awareness into the present. Our motivation is to use this as a gift to ourselves, as a way of taking good care of ourselves, because when we are aware of the present we can appreciate it for exactly what it is, nothing more and nothing less.

Mindfulness of Breath and Body

Some of us will find it helpful to focus on the breath and our body at the same time. Having two things to focus on can be useful for those of us with very active minds. Here we combine mindfulness of the Breath with a Body Scan.

Script: Breath and Body

Start with the 10 Minute Mindfulness of the Breath

1. Now beginning to notice our body.... Keeping some awareness on our breathing as we move most of our attention to noticing our body....

   Perhaps starting with both our feet, and noticing any sensations there.... Contact between the toes... Moisture.... Contact with our sock or stocking... Not trying to do anything more than notice what sensations are there... Then noticing the whole of our feet... Then our ankle and lower leg.... Then our knee and upper leg... Just intending to notice sensations in our body, on the surface or inside... Now noticing our hips...

2. Having an intention to be more aware of our body, moment by moment.... Noticing small body sensations, as well as those that call out for attention.

3. Forming an intention to notice body sensations as they are, not to change anything. Not to create any sense of relaxation.... Just to notice the body as it is.

4. And remembering that whenever we realize our mind has wandered, after some practice this can be understood as a happy moment, as we have just become aware of our thinking again, and can now return to this mindful focus on the present... Just picking up wherever we are in this guided meditation...

5. Now noticing our back, including the full length of our spine.... Now noticing the front of our torso... Now our neck.... Now our head... Let's go into more detail here: Perhaps noticing the contact of our lips, and any muscle tension around our mouth.... Any tension in our jaw... The position of our tongue... Any wetness or taste in our mouth... Noticing our nose and any sensations of warmth or cold as we breathe in and out... Noticing the muscles around our eyes.... Perhaps noticing the contact of our eyelids... Or light coming in through our eyelids... Noticing our forehead.... and the sides of our head... and the ears, and sounds.... and the top and back of our head...

6. Now seeing what is like to notice our body as a whole... Now noticing any part of our body that has discomfort, tension, a sense of holding. Checking in with our breath again... Having some awareness of our breath at the same time as any areas of discomfort in our body. Allowing that to be in our awareness for some breaths without trying to change it. Now shifting our position if that's helpful, to relieve the discomfort. Knowing that if discomfort becomes serious, our first priority is always to our safety and health, so stopping this exercise if that should happen.

7. Now returning our attention to our breathing, then
Noticing sounds...then
Noticing our contact with our chair...

8. Taking one or two more breaths, then opening our eyes and looking around...

And returning to the activities of our day.

Mindfulness of Sounds

When in the city sounds can be great teachers. It is easy to have an attitude towards sounds, liking some, hating others, craving silence. We can work with that. The sounds are great teachers because they help us become aware of our judging minds, always with preferences.

Script: Mindfulness of Sounds

1. Starting by noticing our chair, or, if we are walking, noticing the movement of our feet, as a way of bringing our attention to the present...

2. Now beginning to notice sounds.... Sounds that are strong, and that demand our attention, perhaps.... Also sounds that are faint, that we might miss... Maintaining some awareness of our breathing or our body as we continue to notice sounds....

3. When there are no sounds, just following our breathing...

4. Having the intention just to hear the sounds. When we find ourselves thinking about the sounds giving ourselves a little smile, remembering thinking is what brains do, and returning our attention just to the sounds....

5. We may decide to name them. So..... bird singing, car honking, for example.....

6. Perhaps bringing some curiosity to these sounds. What is their tone? Pitch? Timbre? Other qualities? Then, just noticing these things...

7. As we focus onto sounds, noticing how they arise out of nowhere, fill our consciousness for some time, then fade away....

8. And when we are finished, bringing our attention to our breathing for a moment,... then returning to the activities of our day...

Mindfulness of Thoughts

A lot of what we're doing with mindfulness is changing how we relate to our thoughts.

We're not actively trying to change the thoughts. That's often the content of classical cognitive therapy. In Mindfulness-Based work we're learning to observe the thoughts rather than change them. We're leaning how to observe ourselves having the thoughts. Then they're less 'us' and more something that is happening in us. It's less "I'm a failure," and more "A failure thought is in me," or "A failure thought is here." When we de-center from the thought we can look at it, and have some more freedom in how we respond to it.

We start practicing the 3-Minute Breathing Space, the first step of which is to note what thoughts are currently present in our mind. In this, we are practicing noticing thoughts.

In the meditating instructions, we are following a very special kind of practice. We are not practicing concentration as it is usually taught. Usually the idea in meditation would be that the times

I am noticing the breath are good, and the times my mind has wandered are something I want to change, a work in progress. For us, by contrast, both the focus on breath and the wandering mind are of equal value and interest. When I notice the breath, that's fine, it's my intention. When I notice the mind has wandered I take the attitude of friendly interest in the thought. I note it as "thinking" or I get a little deeper and categorize it as "planning" or "worrying" or "remembering" or " regretting" or any of a bunch of labels which we can make up for ourselves. When we are noting the thought we are not trying to remember it, but rather just to give it a name. Things named are often less fearsome, after all. Once named, things are beginning to be understood. We just note the thought and return to the breath.

Both the breath and the thoughts are useful. They are our teachers.

Script 1: Mindfulness of Thoughts

When thoughts are becoming insistent, rushed, perhaps with an obsessive quality, we can get lost in them. So the first step when we realize this is happening is to take a few breaths with awareness, and to consciously slow down whatever we are doing. Then we can take a look at the thoughts. Are these thoughts part of a frequent pattern of worry or rumination that we have had many times before? Are they on our 'hit list' of negative thoughts, meaning are they patterns we have had many times before, in the past? As these thoughts swim around in our head they can be hard to get a grip on, so we try writing them down; sometimes, when we do that, they can be seen more objectively, because now they are specific. We borrow this from classical cognitive work. Do these thoughts carry emotional content that I am avoiding? What happens if I let those feelings into my awareness and sit with them? The process, then, goes like this:

It can be helpful to practice Mindfulness of Sounds before this meditation.

1. Becoming aware that our thoughts right now are a problem for us

2. Slowing down, as we begin this meditation

3. Asking ourselves, is this part of an ongoing concern, one we've been struggling with for a long time?

4. Are these thoughts on our 'hit list?'

5. Do they carry feelings that I am avoiding?

Each step offers help. When we notice thoughts, we begin to de-center. When we slow down, we send a signal to the brain that things are OK. When we recognize this is a long-term pattern we might realize we do not have to find a solution right now. If the thoughts are on our 'hit list' they may be seen as thoughts rather than as facts. Noticing emotional content, we may stop avoiding the feelings.

Script 2: Mindfulness of Thoughts

It can be helpful to practice Mindfulness of Sounds before this meditation.

1. So now practicing a different way of relating to thoughts.... Instead of returning to the breath, body or sounds when we notice them, now letting them stay in our awareness until they are finished....

2. When we notice a thought, greeting it with awareness that this is what brains do, this is what minds do...

3. So, just following our breath, waiting for a thought to come into awareness...

4. Not trying to create thoughts, but just greeting those that do arise, with a smile of recognition....

5. Perhaps saying to ourselves silently, "Oh here's a thought about _____." Then waiting for it to complete, and returning our awareness of our breathing...

6. So we are just as accepting of our experience when we notice our breathing as we are when we notice we are thinking....

7. Perhaps noticing how thoughts, like sounds, seem to arise out of nowhere, occupy our attention for awhile, then fade away...

8. Just continuing to follow our breath until thoughts appear....

9. When the thoughts spin off into whole stories, relating to them as we have before: giving ourselves a little smile, returning to our breath, knowing this is what brains do. We are interested in thoughts that we can see as thoughts, not so much in spinning them into stories.... When we realize we are lost in a story, returning to our breath.... And when the next thought arises, keeping that intention to let it complete, then returning to our breath...

10. Where is my mind right now?..... and continuing

11. And when we are ready to end this meditation on thoughts.... noticing our chair, noticing sounds, then taking one or two breaths with awareness, then opening our eyes and looking around. And returning to the activities of our day.

Mindfulness of Feelings

We tend to understand feelings in their extremes. When we are angry we know it. When we receive a gift we are really happy, and we know it. When we feel strong emotions like happiness, joy, gratitude, love, anger, shame, frustration, anxiety...we know it.

We believe that we are beings with strong emotions.

But that is not correct.

We have feelings much of the time, we just have tuned them out of our awareness, in the same way that we tune out awareness of our seat, sounds, breath, body and many other things.

In order to know our feelings, we need to be mindful of them.

This is not very hard. All we need do is slow down and set an intention to notice them. We may find one faint feeling, or a jumble of them, or one large one and many small ones. We may find a feeling state that is steady, or that changes breath by breath.

Sometimes, when I meet a new client who lets me know that she is depressed, we explore her history of sadness and build a plan for her treatment. Then I inquire what feelings she is having in that moment of our first appointment. Often the feeling in the moment is not a sad one. We make note of that. She can be a depressed person, and still not be depressed in this moment. Yet, it is significant, this in-the-moment feeling. In future sessions we can explore the non-depressed feelings of this person in different moments. We can learn from them, too.

When we become aware of feelings we may encounter some that we don't like, or that scare us. We would rather not know them. What are we to do? In mindfulness we know the whole of our experience, not just parts we like. It is helpful to remind ourselves, then, that there are no wrong feelings, just wrong actions. I can feel angry, but I will not punch or verbally demean another person, for example.

No wrong feelings, just wrong actions

Working with anxious clients can be interesting as they learn more moment-by-moment awareness of their feelings. Over time many see clearly that when they are anxious it is hard to think straight, to remember things, to find their way to helpful actions. Conversely, when anxiety is down their functioning gets much better. This realization can be quite helpful. They will cut themselves a break when anxiety is high, just waiting for it to stabilize before undertaking challenging tasks.

As anxiety decreases, functioning increases

If we seek a formal practice to become more mindful of our feelings, we might use the Working with Difficulty meditation, available as a track in Dropbox, adding a particular emphasis on feelings. For routine working with feelings we can use Practice #7 in the Quick Start guide.

Mindful Listening

When we apply mindfulness to the act of listening, a new way presents itself.

Usually, we listen and at the same time we process what we are hearing. Do we agree? What is this person getting at? Is this useful for us? How should we respond when they stop speaking? We hate this, how can we get this person to stop? Why are we feeling this way? Simply put, we usually think and analyze while we are listening. Now we can try listening, but without engaging the mind in thoughts, just taking it in.

This way listens just to hear, listens just so the other person can be heard, can know she is being heard, can feel known.

At first we may find that this mindful listening is scary. Will we know what to say when they finish speaking? But this way of listening may have a positive impact on our concentration. Do you see how hard it must be to listen and analyze at the same time? Yet for many it is a habit because there seems to be a payoff: We congratulate ourselves on the skill of our response, or the person seems to appreciate it. It may be really hard to slow down our thinking mind and just listen. This wouldn't be a practice if it were easy! The way we listen may be a long-established habit.

Trying it, we may be surprised: When it is our turn to speak, we may intuitively know how to respond. After all, our sub-conscious is still at work, and thinking can be a rather rapid process. We may find that in the few seconds between when the speaker stops and when we frame a response, things might become clear for us. If not, we can always ask a clarifying question, such as, "Could you speak a little more about that?"

Or, we realize we can pause awhile and just take in what we have been hearing. In a way we have been softening and opening to this other person as we have been listening.

There is a good chance the other person has sensed this, from our facial expression or body language. It is genuine. It helps the other person to soften and open to our response. It is a very different way of listening and conversing. Our mindful listening can change the experience for the other person, even if the other person doesn't intend to change at all. Softening and opening with acceptance, while listening mindfully, can be an act of compassion.

When we are listening this way we are more likely to be in touch with our gentle, feeling, self, our vulnerable self. With this awareness our response can have elements of our feeling selves in it. Mindful listening is healing for us, healing for others.

With softening and opening to all of experience, we learn to be gentle with ourselves, to accept ourselves as we are. We also find ourselves more able to listen mindfully, to focus on taking in what the other is saying to us, learning to be gentle to ourselves and to know that the right response will come to us.

Exercise: Practice listening mindfully

We can try each of these ways, realizing their differences:

-Try listening without thinking.
-Try listening while at the same time noticing our breathing.
-Then try listening while at the same time that noticing our body.
-Then try listening while at the same time noticing our feelings.

Experiment: which is best for us?

Introducing Mindful Listening to clients

To be introduced after the client has learned how to relate to thoughts that crop up during meditation

Script: Mindful listening, group setting

Therapist: One way to practice mindfulness is with mindful listening. With mindful listening we give our thinking a break, we simply listen without thinking, without thinking of what our response will be, without thinking about whether we agree or disagree, without thinking about what is on our to-do list...

This can be challenging at first. We may fear we won't know what to say when the person stops speaking. We may fear that we are giving over control of ourselves to that person by being complacent. We may fear being dominated.

How about you give it a try while I keep talking?

Therapist: (Just keeps talking for a minute or two.) OK, how was that for you?

Client 1: I felt scared.

Client 2: I felt like I had power

Client 3: It was easy. I felt my body relaxing

Therapist: That brings up a good point. Sometimes mindful listening is easier when we hold our body in awareness, or when we follow our breathing. Does one of those appeal to you? Let's try it

Discuss: Most often clients find it helpful to notice their body as they are listening without thinking. Many find they are able to retain more, and feel more in control.

At this point we have an idea of a range of mindfulness meditations to help us and our clients become more aware of the present. Now we will move on to the next phase: allowing our awareness to continue, not chasing it away.

CHAPTER FOUR

Allowing:
We Learn a New Way
to Relate to Pain

I am checking my phone. The text message says Thomas is dying. He is in Dallas with his partner. Last night he had a massive stroke. Is barely alive, not expected to live out the weekend. My heart sinks. I have known him 45 years. I go to the couch and sit. The feelings are strong. So, so sad. I feel my energy leaving me. I imagine I am sitting by his bed, I remember being with him. He was a healer, and I admired him. He healed the poor in Texas.

My feelings become too much to bear. I realize my thoughts are feeding my feelings, and move my attention from the thoughts to my body. The feelings of heaviness and sadness remain the same, and I become aware of a tightness in my throat, a cramped feeling in the back of my head, a pre-cry feeling that spreads down into my chest. I don't particularly want these feelings, but I realize it will be best to let these feelings take their course. I sit with them. After a while the feelings diminish and I begin thinking of Thomas again. The feelings intensify so I sit with them more.

There are things to do. I do them. The sadness is there, and I can bear it, I have sat with it.

A few days later I call a client who missed a session. "I had a stroke," he says. Thomas' stroke flashes into my mind. We speak, and after I get off the phone I feel unable to continue what I've been doing. I feel sort of glum, like there are more feelings than I'm aware of. I don't want to pick up my pen. I realize I need to sit with this.

I go to the couch and sit. I intend to sit for 20 minutes, but really don't know how long I'll need. As I sit I feel really intense feelings of sadness arising in me. I don't get numb, so this is workable, but the feelings are really strong. I make an effort to feel what is going on in my body. There is tightness in my throat, then a clenching there, followed by a feeling of *emptiness in my stomach and low energy, almost a faintness, then my attention goes back to my constricted throat, then something happens in the back of my head, a sort of tightness like my brain is being squeezed, then my throat again, and stomach. After some time I notice my shoulders relax... I hadn't known they were tight.*

The emptiness and throat sensations are still present, but less so. My mind starts to wander. I intentionally bring Thomas back to mind, to continue my work of sitting-with. The feelings intensify, but not as much. I have some pleasant memories. I slip off into a light sleep. I am allowing these uncomfortable feelings to be in me, I am sitting with them.

Experiential Avoidance

Steven Hayes developed the idea that some kinds of mental illness can be seen as coming from a cause; he posited this could clarify things more than defining mental illness based only on symptoms. This idea works really well for a constellation of disorders that have in common experiential avoidance. So, for example, when we think of sadness we may see an attempt to avoid pain, often emotional pain. A depressed person may struggle to avoid thinking about the loss, the trauma, the shame that seem to have caused the depression, hoping that not thinking about it will let the pain go away. Unfortunately, for many this does not work, and spirals of negative thinking just become more tenacious.

An anxious person may try to avoid thinking about the source of anxiety, possibly a worry about employment, a worry about love, a worry about health, because thinking of those things causes emotional pain. Unfortunately, for many this does not work, as the thoughts intrude into awareness again and again, and painful emotions come along with them. The same attempting-to-avoid can be said for other emotional ailments, such as PTSD, obsessive thoughts, grief, the dissociative disorders, anger, and social anxiety.

The presence of all this experiential avoidance may be invisible until we consciously decide to have a look at it, to study it, to know it.

Let's start by thinking through how our clients might react to the idea of allowing the unpleasant to remain in awareness.

We May Find Resistance to this Allowing

Once we become aware, we find that we like some of what we notice, while we would rather not know about other parts. This presents a problem. Our senses and our minds are not able to put on blinders, and only be aware of what we want to notice.

We may have a habit of trying to avoid pain. Few of us would notice a headache and say to ourselves, "Let me feel it," without some very good reason. We may reach for a pill, a pain reliever. We may be drawn to a pill that announces it takes effect in 15 minutes, rather than 30, because we don't want this pain go to on any longer than necessary. We may distract ourselves until the pain goes away, because it is so unpleasant.

This wish for the pain to go away, and the urge to be unaware of it until it does, is normal. We are pain-avoiding creatures. But this wish not to experience, to not know, has consequences. It turns out to be quite hard to "'not know" something that is staring us in the face. Pushing anything out of awareness can be difficult. If I say the words "Polar Bear" and ask that we keep those words out of our awareness, we may find it quite difficult. Try it. This is not a small teaching. It was first used by PD Ouspensky in the 1930's. Lots of energy can be expended trying to keep things out of our mind. Often, when we try, those ideas only gain in strength as some perverse mechanism of mind will not let them go.

Thinking as a Defense Against Feeling

There are some things we do in life that can be normal and helpful, but with a small, subtle shift can become defenses against feeling. Defenses against emotional pain might be quite invisible, until we begin to perceive them through our practice of mindfulness.

We may come to realize that some of our thinking is an avoidance of feeling. While we don't actively try to keep thinking, we may find thinking is a force with its own energy. The mind sometimes likes to produce thoughts, lots of them, fast, with few gaps between them. Thinking this way can be a way to avoid emotional pain.

We may spend a lot of time worrying. Caught up in thought this way can be a way of trying to find a solution to the emotional pain, thus avoiding directly feeling it.

We may spend a lot of time ruminating about the past, thinking of regrets. While this may bring a certain amount of pain into awareness, it may not let the full force of emotional pain in. This also can be a defense against emotional pain.

We may be surprised at how this avoidance of negative feelings plays out in our lives. When we have a sad feeling, we may resist feeling it; we may try to think of something happy. When we feel worried we may start searching for ways to reduce the worry; we may try talking to ourselves, going over all the reasons we should not feel worried.

We may try to push out of awareness various bodily sensations that we associate with feelings. Perhaps we have pain in our lower back. Perhaps we are aware of wrinkles on our faces. Unconscious attempts to avoid this awareness isolate us from our own bodies and from our moment-by-moment felt experiences.

Perhaps we have sexual sensations we would rather not have. Perhaps we feel tired after walking up some steps. If we have a habit of blocking emotional pain out of awareness, we may see and hear a couple arguing and just watch and listen, without feeling anything consciously. We may see a homeless person and feel little or nothing. We may be criticized and feel nothing.

We may live with blinders so invisible that we are not aware how actively we are avoiding emotional pain. We may notice that a lot of things that would normally create some emotional pain in us do not. We guess that there are worried or sad feelings inside us, but we do not feel them. Moments like these may have a dissociative feel to them. These moments may have a functional feel: after all we can't go along everyday feeling everything.

As a result of living like this, cut off from important feelings, we may feel isolated. We may have difficulty connecting with other people. We may feel disconnected from life around us. We may feel lonely. We may not actually experience important parts of our lives.

In mindfulness it may be helpful to think of this general phenomenon as pushing away experience, as experiential avoidance. Clinically, it may be a form of dissociation.

The Mouse in the Maze Experiment

One way of understanding the cost of this aversion is to think of this experiment. Two groups of college students were given a paper maze with the assignment of starting in the center and finding a route out of the maze. All the students were asked to imagine they were a mouse trying to get out of the maze.

The first group was given a maze in which they were trying to get out so that the mouse could get a tasty piece of cheese. This represented a sort of moving towards or welcoming experience, as one would in mindfulness.

The second group was given a maze in which they were trying to get away from an owl perched in a nearby tree. When they got out they would be safe in their nest. This represented a sort of avoidance, the getting away from something that we have been discussing.

All the students successfully completed the maze. This experiment did not stop there. After doing the maze, both groups were given a test for creativity. This short maze experience, in which one group welcomed experience and the other group tried to avoid experience, had very different results. The "welcoming" group had creativity scores that were 50% higher than those of the "avoiding" group. We can understand that the creative mind is free to think widely, and the uncreative mind might be constricted, with narrow perspective. Imagine what the impact might be over a lifetime lived with either a "welcoming" or "avoiding" habit.

Three Attitudes
We Have for Experience

After some practice with noticing all our experience, we may realize that we have attitudes about close to everything. It may be helpful to think of these attitudes in 3 major groups:

Grasping: Liking, wanting to hold onto, wanting to keep, afraid to lose. We tend to grasp at pleasurable experience.

Aversive: Not liking, wanting to stay away from, wanting to push away. We tend to be aversive to unpleasant experience.

Confused: Unsure, maybe even unaware.

Note: With mindfulness we try to recognize these attitudes, but not necessarily to change them. Each can be used wisely, or badly.

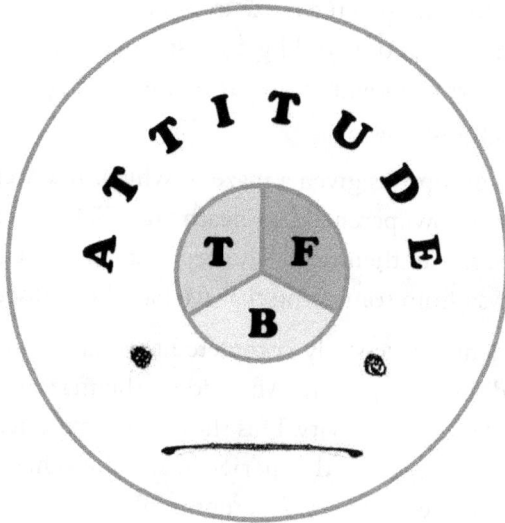

Illustration: It turns out we have attitude around just about everything.

When we first become aware of aversion, and attitude in general, we are surprised at how much of our experience these attitudes encompass. Note: we use T for thoughts, F for feelings, and B for body.

We Use Exposure to Build Tolerance for Intense Experience

If we and our clients are moving towards becoming more aware of intense feelings, we need to prepare. We begin to build tolerance so we can handle stronger experience without becoming overwhelmed. We can do this through gradual exposure to difficult situations.

When we have learned emotional tolerance, we can expose ourselves to the feared element, whether it is sadness, anxiety, anger, obsessive thinking, attention deficit or one of a host of possibilities, and we can prevent becoming overwhelmed by learning to do this gradually, introducing just the amount of discomfort that we can tolerate in the process of exposure.

Traditionally, we try to reduce the pain. We start with difficulties, and we help remove the difficulties to reduce the pain. Or we help the client process the feelings, so the pain is gone. Now we have another approach. We build tolerance of difficult feelings, so that when we encounter them, we can bear them.

> We have a choice: reduce the pain, or increase tolerance for the pain.

One of the things we learn as we practice mindfulness is that our experience keeps changing. Taking a pause and checking in, we might notice anxious feelings, some thoughts about our ability to write, a sense of tightness in our belly, a slight sense of nausea, along with muscle clenching at the jaw. We have learned that if we pause again in 10 minutes, we might have a very different internal experience. Over time we learn that all our experience goes in waves, one moment unpleasant, another moment neutral/confusing, another moment pleasant. Knowing that an unpleasant feeling state may not last a long time is helpful as we learn to endure these feelings.

With allowing, we help clients feel the reality of their feelings without becoming overwhelmed. Allowing and gradual exposure go hand–in–hand.

One way to practice allowing is with a second version of the 3-Minute Breathing Space. In this version we adjust some details so that it helps us de-center a bit from intensity. It also it gives us a way to introduce and practice allowing. It is called the 3-Minute Breathing Space-Coping.

3-Minute Breathing Space: Coping

The 3-Minute Breathing Space - Coping is for use when upset is large enough that we want to look more deeply into the situation. It is similar to the regular 3-Minute Breathing Space, with the addition of some extra grounding material in each step. The first step is modified to help us de-center from the thoughts. The second step is modified to help us focus on the breath. the third step is modified to practice staying with physical discomfort. Some people will want to make this their norm.

Exercise: Practice the 3-Minute Breathing Space: Coping. This is included in the Dropbox tracks.

Script: 3-Minute Breathing Space: Coping

First, drawing our attention to our experience in the present, doing a 3-Way Check-in: noticing our thoughts... noticing our feelings... and noticing whatever body sensations come into awareness... Then saying to ourselves something like, "a _____ thought is here," and "a feeling of _____ is here," and "a sense of _____ is in my body." So, now we are aware of our present experience, our thoughts, feelings, and body sensations, and maybe a bit de-centered from them.

Second, focusing this awareness of the present down to one particular point in our body, by bringing our attention to the movement of our breath in our belly. The slight expansion of our belly on the in-breath, and the slight falling away on the out-breath. Perhaps anchoring our attention on our breathing by counting out-breaths, something like, "In one, out one, in two, out two, in three..." for about a minute.

Third, expanding this awareness of the breath in our belly out to an awareness of our whole body. We may scan around our body as we do this, asking ourselves if there is any place in our body where there is discomfort, holding, tightness.

Then noting the location of discomfort, and practicing bringing our attention right into that area, sort of breathing into that area, allowing our attention to stay there for a few breaths. As we do so saying to ourselves something like, "It's already here, I might as well feel it," and having a sense that we can open to this experience of discomfort, and soften our response to it.

There is another step available after this, which will be described in the chapter on action.

And then returning to the activities of our day

Illustration: The 3-Minute Breathing Space: Coping

We modify the regular 3-Minute Breathing Space, de-centering from our experience, and then we notice any aversion to

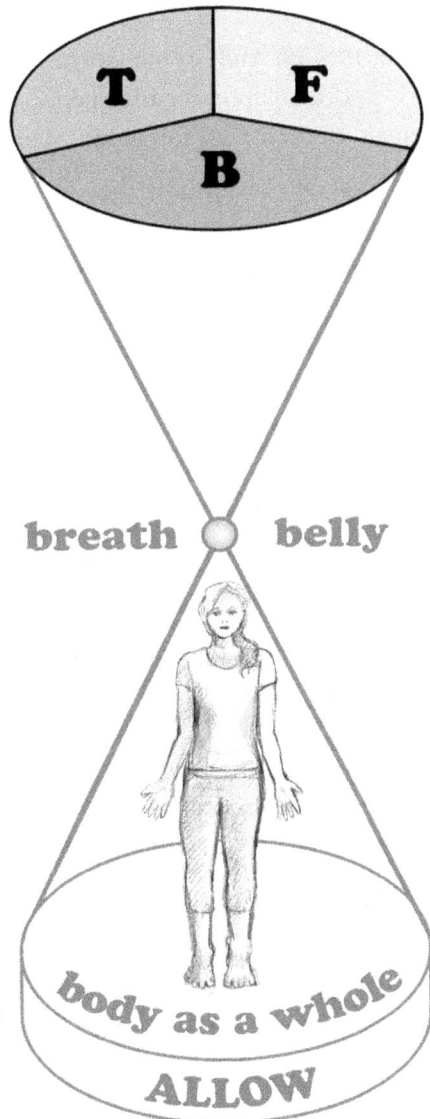

T **F**

B

breath ◯ belly

body as a whole

ALLOW

physical discomfort, allowing it to stay in our awareness. Note: we use T for thoughts, F for feelings, and B for body.

Practicing Allowing in Therapy Sessions

While we are with our clients, after we have done a pause, or helped the client with a 3-Way Check-in, a full 3-Minute Breathing Space, or the 4-Right Nows, we have a choice.

We may go back to our normal therapy process, or we may feel it would be helpful for the client to allow these perceptions to remain in awareness for awhile. We can call this process "allowing."

We ask our client how they feel about this, about sitting with feelings they have noticed in the present. This helps us gauge their sense of strength in the moment. If it is OK we may slow things down, ask that they also bring some attention to their breath, perhaps noticing it in their belly. After some time we inquire again about their experience in the moment. We acknowledge that. We notice some more breaths. Perhaps we comment on the steadiness or changeability of this short stream of check-ins, depending on the client's experience.

This allowing can be a helpful way for clients to learn about themselves. It can be helpful for building emotional tolerance. It can be helpful for processing feelings.

Case Example:
Allowing Feelings to Remain, Even Though They are Already Strong

Claire is angry at her employer for reducing services to the needy. She talks about how she feels, has tears, keeps talking. I ask if we can let the anger just be there, let the thinking take a short break, let the feelings just be in her, for a bit, and notice what's happening in her body? She complies, allows the feelings, and in a minute starts to speak of her employer again.

I ask if she can sit with the anger a bit longer, can she put the thought on hold? Claire agrees. What feelings are in you right now, I ask. She reports feeling some frustration, sadness, and disappointment. I ask how it is in her body, and she reports discomfort in her chest. We stay with that. After allowing these feelings to just be in her awhile we discuss the experience, then we go back to her talk therapy.

Feelings Flowing

Clients may wonder about this approach. They may have a habit of trying to avoid emotional pain. It may help to give clients a visual picture that dramatizes the difficulty of stopping the flow of feelings.

Sometimes feelings are so strong we just want them to stop. They flow into us like a poisonous fluid, sometimes even spinning us off into panic. They are like a river that won't stop. We imagine building a dam to stop the flow, but the continuing rise of pressure keeps breaking through the dam.

So we try something else. We abandon the dam. Instead we see ourselves as a rock in the river of feelings flowing in us. As a rock in the river, the feelings just flow around us. There are just as many feelings as when we tried to build a dam, but now they flow around us. They are painful, even sometimes very strong, but they do not stop in us, they continue to flow through us and out of us. We realize we can tolerate this, and we remember that feelings feel like they'll last forever, but they don't. At some point they have diminished, or not, and we get on with our lives. Illustration: Allowing feelings to flow

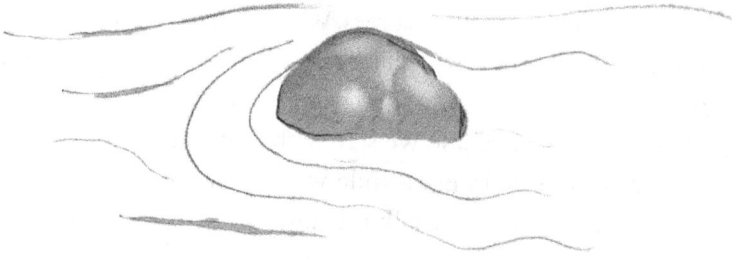

Illustration: Allowing feelings to flow

We can build a dam, and try to stop the river of feelings, or we can see ourselves as a rock, the feelings flowing around us.

Maintaining Perspective During the Process of Allowing

Some understandings can be helpful as we work with the process of allowing. They arise out of practice with the 3-Way Check-in, and are helpful in moments when experience becomes intense. With these understandings, it becomes easier to maintain perspective, to not get lost in the intensity. They are understandings of thoughts, feelings, and body sensations.

Thoughts are not facts: We realize that a lot of our mental process is not too important. That we spend a lot of time needlessly ruminating, dreaming, fantasizing, worrying, planning. That our thoughts influence our moods; that our moods influence our thoughts. Many thoughts are not a solid as they appear.

Feelings are not forever: We realize that we may have feelings all the time. We used to be aware of feelings only when something strong happened, like receiving a gift or stubbing our toe. But now we learn that feelings are present most of the time. That's not all. We learn that they change frequently, sometimes seemingly with a will of their own. We learn that feelings, while present, often feel like they will last forever, while in fact, they can change quickly and often.

Body pain is not everywhere: When we have a toothache, we are miserable. But as we become more body-focused we learn that it is not everywhere, that pain is local, that other parts of our body are perfectly fine. We learn to find the edges of the pain, and we get to know its character: what color it would be; what weight it would be; what it would it sound like; if it had color, what would that be? When we locate the pain, we acknowledge there are parts of ourselves that are pain-free.

Teaching story:
Remaining calm in the face of shifting experience.

A man lived on a farm, with his son. One day a horse wandered onto the farm, out of the woods, with no owner. And he kept it. The neighbors said, "What good luck," but the farmer said nothing. Weeks later the man's son was riding the horse, fell off, and broke his leg. The neighbors said, "What bad luck," but the farmer said nothing. Weeks later the local army enlister came by, seizing all the able-bodied young men to go fight in a bloody war. He saw the boy had a broken leg, and left him with his father. The neighbors said, "What good luck." but the farmer said nothing.

***Moral**: some things appear bad, others good, but we really don't know.*

With mindfulness we learn to direct our attention in various ways. We have probably practiced keeping our attention on each area of internal experience (thoughts, feelings, body sensations) and of external experience (the 5 senses). Through doing pauses, we may have noticed how thoughts often lead to feelings, and feelings often lead to thoughts. When we are in a feelings-thoughts loop, and they are negative, feelings can rapidly escalate. They feed each other. On the other hand, when we direct our attention away from thoughts and towards feelings and body sensations we may not experience as much escalation, perhaps none at all. Body sensations and feelings do not feed each other nearly as much. When we rest our experience in body-feelings awareness, we may find more stability than when we rest our experience in thoughts-feelings awareness.

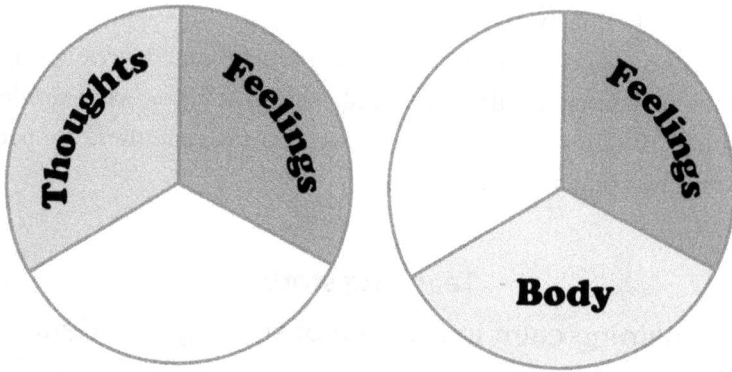

Illustration: Aware of Thoughts/Feelings
vs. Aware of Feelings/Body

Feelings and thoughts together can feed each other, and feelings can escalate. Feelings and body awareness can allow feelings to flow through, without escalating them.

Stuck in the rain with no umbrella

Allowing in action might look like this. Say we are coming upstairs from the subway, and we see that what was a blue sky has turned dark, and it is raining. Because the sky had been blue we did not bring an umbrella. Now, our clothing may get damaged by the rain. We look around for an umbrella vendor, and see none. At this moment we take a breath and realize we have a choice. We can go out into the rain cursing it and our own idiocy (that might be our normal way) or we could go into the rain with an attitude born of allowing, an attitude that it's already here and there's nothing I can do to change it, I can't push it away. In this second way, we might walk out into the rain with curiosity, noticing our heavy feelings in the body, noticing the feel of the raindrops on our face, the sound of the raindrops on our clothing. We might even tell ourselves, if we have been practicing awhile, "Wow, this is really interesting...."

With mindfulness we also are building a habit of working in the present, rather than in the past or future. So when we build tolerance for strong feeling states, we do it in the present, without the escalations that can happen when thinking of the past or future. For example, we may be feeling anxiety about our financial situation. We notice our experience in the present, right now, with the 3 internals and shifting attention towards body and feelings.

A Process for Moving From Avoidance to Allowing

We may want to go through a process of steps to build tolerance for experience.

1. We may start by realizing just how much of our lives are lived without awareness of the present. We might eat something as we did in the Raisin Exercise (a raisin, a cranberry, a cracker, anything) very slowly, noticing the 5 senses as we do so. Afterwards reflecting on how much experience we miss out on when we're on automatic pilot.

2. We may intentionally notice nice things that happen to us, or around us, noticing things that are pleasant, taking care to develop the skill of noticing internal and external experience – just as we did with the Events Calendar. For example, we might hear the wind in the trees and note what we saw, what we heard, what we smelled, what the wind felt like on our face, any tastes that were present. Moving to internal experience, we might note the thought we had as we heard the wind in the trees, what feelings we had, and what we felt in our body.

3. When we are ready, we may start intentionally noticing unpleasant things, using the same process as for pleasant things in step 2. For example, smelling unpleasant things, we notice external and internal experience.

4. We may then make a study of aversion/avoidance in our lives, noticing what we try to avoid, and how that goes for us. We

may need to make a special effort to notice the things we avoid unconsciously, such as certain memories or feelings. We can do this by slowing down and becoming aware of our attitude towards each thing we notice, each thing that happens. Do we like it, want more of it? Do we dislike it, want it to go away? Are we confused by it, uncomfortable, not sure? There are many ways to practice with this One way is with mindfulness of sounds while we are meditating. How do we relate to them?

5. Then, as life unfolds, we might make a point of noticing when unpleasant things happen or difficult feelings arise, noticing related aversions and staying with those feelings despite our inclination not to. If they become overwhelming we move from thoughts-feelings awareness to body-feeling awareness; there is no need to spin out into panic. The 3-Minute Breathing Space can be helpful here, as can the 4-Right Nows or the pause.

6. After developing a degree of experience and comfort, we might try going a big step further, actually introducing unpleasant things into our awareness, noticing our internal experience, and staying with that experience for as long as it is tolerable. For example, if we know we have negative feelings about a friendship, we consciously think of that, allowing the feelings to develop, and stay in us, as long as this is not traumatic. If we do sense the feelings are getting too strong, we revert to body-feelings awareness or, if necessary, distraction. The Working With Difficulty exercise can be helpful for this.

7. We gradually increase the intensity of our exposure. If awareness of a bad job review causes a small upset we may start there, some time later moving up to imagining a formal warning, some time after that moving up to imagining a personal layoff.

In this process of gradually moving towards what we avoid, we are holding in mind the idea that there is a level of upset which is small, even insignificant, another level which is somewhat uncomfortable and with which we can practice, and yet another level which is too intense, that we are not yet ready to work on. We plan our exposure so that we have enough feelings, but not too much.

Monitoring Feelings: Ways to Increase or Decrease Focus on Them

We are holding in mind that there is a graduated group of responses we can make. For example, we may rest in knowing the upsetting thought and related feelings and body sensations, or we may move attention to the body and feelings, or we may move our attention to just the breath, or to the sensations of breath in the body, or to external experience, or even to thought stopping.

Thought Stopping

We can use thought stopping if we are becoming overwhelmed. It is the practice of distraction in which we fill the mind with neutral material taken from the external environment right in front of us. In thought stopping, we might describe in detail and out loud, the patterns in the rug in front of us, for example.

Managing Exposure

It may be that our feelings get close to overwhelming during this work, but that we are able to catch this. In these cases, we can practice doing the work of allowing, and when the feelings get towards too much intensity, stopping, directing our attention outside of ourselves (as in thought stopping, above), then returning to the focus of attention after the feelings have calmed enough that it feels safe. We can go back and forth in this way as we gradually increase our ability to tolerate the feelings.

In deciding how fast to move in this process we want to be aware of the amount of trauma that has happened and how we have dealt with that so far. Do we use avoidance? Dissociation? Has it been buried in our unconscious? Have there been indications that bringing up these memories may be traumatic? Have we invested time working with or allowing these feelings? The more repressed or dissociated, the more careful, the more patient, we are.

There will be questions of how fast to jump in and deal with avoided feelings or situations. A good, general approach is to be kind, and sensitive, and to go slow.

Introducing Difficulties into Awareness

We have been exploring ways to allow ourselves and our clients to be with their experience, rather than continuing to avoid it. In some cases we will want to help a client along a path of recovery more actively, by putting together a controlled process for healing through allowing.

In work with Post-Traumatic Stress Disorder, for example, this may be a way forward. When clients have learned ways to stabilize themselves as feelings move towards becoming overwhelming, we can begin to introduce difficulties into awareness. Each week we can guide our client towards stronger feelings, as they have learned to increase their tolerance. Eventually the client will be able to feel traumatic feelings without becoming overwhelmed, and will be better prepared to go on with life.

Exercise: Practice Working with Difficulties. This is included in the Dropbox tracks.

Case Example: Working with Difficulty Through Allowing

We have been working on anxiety about taking a test. We decide to experiment, to practice allowing the anxiety to be present in session.

Therapist: How is your anxiety right now?

John: I don't know, pretty strong

Therapist: Do you feel it in your body?

John: My stomach is a little unsettled. (Therapist decides this is a tolerable, workable amount.)

Therapist: It can be helpful to focus on these feelings, right now. Could we give that a try, see how that is for you? (Therapist. feels the level is comfortable, but we check to get the client's perception, also.)

John: Sure

Therapist: It will help if you can close your eyes, or just soft focus them on a spot on the rug a few feet in front of you. That way there are fewer distractions. Is that ok? (If there is sufficient safety in the room, we also close our eyes, and let the client know.)

John: OK

Therapist: OK, let's start by helping you focus on the present. Can you feel your contact with the chair, right now? What's that like?

John: It feels soft

Therapist: Let's continue to focus on the present, by paying attention to your body. Just noticing whatever comes into awareness.

Therapist: And now, just noticing your breath, your in-breaths and your out-breaths.

Therapist: Let's continue with this, paying attention to sounds. So, just listening to sounds, sounds nearby, sounds from outside, even sounds we might not usually pay attention to, just noting them in your mind, no need to say them out loud.

Therapist: And now bringing to mind the test you're worried about, letting thoughts of it rest in your awareness, perhaps in the form of one or two sentences.

Therapist: Noticing any feelings, meaning emotions, that are coming up, just noting them silently for yourself.

Therapist: (After a short time has passed) Now saying out loud any feelings you are noticing. (We check in, wanting the feelings to be significant but not overwhelming.)

John: I feel some worry. I can handle it, it's not overwhelming, but I can really feel it.

Therapist: Now checking in with your body, scanning around for any areas of discomfort, tightness, un-ease.

Therapist: Now picking one of those areas in your body that has the most discomfort and bringing your attention right into that area. Allowing yourself to feel the discomfort in your body. Perhaps noticing your breathing as you hold your attention there. Often we avoid discomfort. Now, doing the opposite, really allowing yourself to feel it, to stay with it in your awareness. (Here building tolerance through allowing.)

Therapist: How is it for you right now? Please tell me out loud.

John: My throat feels a little bit tight.

Therapist: Is it ok to keep your attention on that tightness a little bit longer?

John: OK

Therapist: OK, that was good. Now moving your attention gradually back to the present, so, noticing your contact with the chair again, noticing sounds, then taking one or two more breaths, then opening your eyes and looking around.

A discussion of the experience follows. Therapist wants to figure out if the exposure can be increased next time, or any other adjustments that might help. Exposure can be increased by longer focus, or by bringing stronger material to mind.

Working with Allowing, Less Formally

After practicing with this for some time, we may be more comfortable with generalizing the practice and working with it less formally, without using the complete steps listed above, or the complete Working with Difficulty audio track. We make a plan with our client, we practice gradual exposure to the intense material over a number of sessions. Each time we learn how much is enough to work with, and sometimes we learn how much is too much, and slow down the process. We may learn that we need to speed up if the client isn't feeling much. We may learn that we need to slow down because the client momentarily dissociates, by client report, or by our own sense of the client's well being.

Case Example: Allowing as the Center of a Session

Avery had a really difficult childhood. He was emotionally and physically abused until he left home, and even after, when he visited as an adult. When he thought about the things that happened, he often became overwhelmed. He actively tried to keep much of this out of his awareness. He found it difficult to concentrate. He had trouble keeping friends. His symptoms were those of post-traumatic stress disorder, PTSD.

We were working with his PTSD. He had established safety with his therapist. He had learned mindfulness and breathing to stay present when his feelings were strong, and we were slowly helping him re-introduce memories into awareness so that he did not re-traumatize himself.

For this session, he came in with news that his older brother told him of an event he didn't remember, something that happened earlier than his other memories. His brother told him that once, while his father had been beating Avery, his mother had intervened, at which point his father transferred his anger to his Mom. Avery practiced pausing with me, as he recounted this. He was aware of feeling frightened, sad, and vulnerable. The he felt numb. We explored that, and understood that his feelings had become so intense that he could not tolerate them, so he had dissociated from them, had become numb.

Together we helped him bring his awareness fully into the present. We paused, did a 3-Way Check-in of his thoughts, feelings and body sensations in that very moment. We followed the breath for awhile, as Avery remained numb.

After perhaps 5 minutes, Avery told me he was beginning to experience very strong feelings, like fear, and sadness, and guilt. He was back from the numbness, there was something for us to work with, so we continued, slowly.

We discussed the idea that feelings seem to be forever while they are in us, but that actually they often evolve moment by moment. Tears flowed. I asked if he was comfortable with sitting with them, or if perhaps they felt like too much for right now. He signaled he was okay with this. I thought of this as exposure to his trauma.

We frequently did the 3-Way Check-in. So, while a past event was present, we related to it via his present experience of thoughts, feelings and body sensations. This helped him keep grounded.

As he stayed with the feelings in his body, I found some of these feelings in my own body, noticing that my throat constricted, my chest felt heavy my stomach tense. So it was really "we" sitting with this.

Time passed. Avery at times closed his eyes, at times opened them. I monitored him closely. He had not "left the room," was not lost in the experience. He was okay. Avery then told me the feelings were decreasing in intensity, and asked what should we do now? It occurred to me that he was feeling very vulnerable. In a sense he was adult Avery, but also he was Avery the very vulnerable child processing something that happened when he was young, small, and unprotected. We explored an experiment: helping that little child in Avery, at that moment. By keeping the adult Avery with that little child he could stay with the feelings, be accepting of what was, and by staying with all that he would be practicing love for the child, rather than pushing him back out of awareness, and since the child was really a part of him, Avery would be practicing self-love.

I asked Avery to imagine that the little child was him standing in front of himself. I asked that he consider what he would like to do. Avery wanted to hug him, to kiss him and stroke his hair, to speak comforting words to him. This continued for a while.

With just a little time left, I asked Avery if we could release the child that was him, at least for now, and he felt at peace with that. We did the 3-Way Check in. He had a lot of feelings in him, and felt quite exhausted. We practiced feeling the feelings in his body, reducing the feedback-loop between thoughts and feelings, and spoke about actions he might take after the session. I reminded him to take extra good care of himself after he left, since he had been through an intense experience. We thought of some helpful actions, agreed that he would do frequent 3-Way Check-ins, stopping to meditate or do something mindfully when he felt it would be helpful.

In this session, we built on Avery's ability to focus on the present via his breath, his previous experience of sitting with strong emotions, his understanding that feelings tend to change and don't last forever. We used the pause, the 3-Way Check-in, exposure, self-love in his caring for the child within him, and we used the idea of wise action to plan his activities after session. Using these tools we moved seamlessly between present focused therapy and more traditional methods.

CHAPTER FIVE

Accepting: Maybe We Can Live With This

*L*ying in my bed, sleepless at 4 am, I realized that there was nothing I could do to get to sleep. This sleeplessness had been going on for weeks. I was defeated. And a lightness came over me. A sense of being not so defeated after all. If I couldn't change this, I would just have to adapt to it. I felt like singing. I was tempted to wake my wife in jubilation, but resisted. It was 4 am, after all.

I am sleepless for weeks at a time, when I catch a cold or get my nose allergies. It all started 30 years ago when I walked through a field of uncut Timothy grass in June, and was immersed in pollen. Something in my body said, "No!" and my nose started running, my body sneezing. Every summer this happened. I got shots, they didn't help... I was untreatable. I blew my nose a lot, what else can you do when it's like a leaky faucet? A few years ago a doc looked inside my nose and said, "You've got polyps." The result of all that nose blowing. Other docs agreed, but taking them out wouldn't help, they would just grow back. So I began a life of being a little bit crazy about not catching cold or exposing myself to grass pollen. But I couldn't control this, despite my best efforts. Pollen is very good at spreading in the air. Catching cold is hard to avoid in a crowded city. I suffered often.

I had been painfully aware of my sleeplessness, and the difficulty of doing anything about it. I was mildly obsessed about finding a solution.

Nothing helped until that moment of realization that I was defeated, I had to accept my condition. With that defeat all the forces in me that were saying, "You have to change this," were no longer needed. They lost their force, because I accepted that I could not change it. Waking to the fact of my sleeplessness I realized I had a rough road ahead of me. I would need naps, *coffee, tea, a lighter schedule during the weeks I couldn't sleep. But I could and would cope. Emotionally, I moved from a sense of hopelessness, often a factor in depression, to a sense of hope. In terms of mindfulness, I was ready to allow the sleeplessness to be present, to lie in bed and be with it, rather than hating it, wanting to be rid of it, feeling aversive to it.*

My experience of frustration with sleeplessness was strong. I wanted sleep, I needed sleep. I exhausted all the methods I could think of to improve my sleep. Still, I judged myself for not sleeping well. I needed something to change. Only when I progressed to acceptance was I able to see a way forward.

Acceptance in mindfulness involves a shift in perspective in which we change from fighting something to a sense that we can live with it; that we don't always have to be fighting to change it. We may have grown comfortable with the situation, or we may not like it at all, but we realize we could live with it, and be relieved of the sense that we must change it. Along with this change in perspective we might experience a sense of relief. It may come in a flash, as happened for me around the issue of non-sleeping, or we may go through a period of being in acceptance for awhile, losing it, and getting it back.

....
Acceptance: a sense that we could live with the difficulty we have.
....

One way to look at suffering is that it involves essential pain plus pain added by us. For example, when I stub my toe, I feel real pain in my toe, it stings, the bone hurts, it feels squeezed as it swells, I may feel some blood. That is the essential pain, something real and felt in my body. Then there is the rest of the pain that is added on when I start berating myself for being clumsy, for being a mindfulness teacher and still not paying attention to what's immediately in front of me, for not being more careful. Perhaps I add some thoughts about how I could do something even more serious next time, like step off the curb and be hit by a car. That's the pain that's added by me. We can think of it as being two arrows. The first arrow is the pain in my toe, the second is launched by me at me in my reactions to the accident. Part of what can peel away with acceptance is the pain of the second arrow.

In medicine there is a realization that someone in bad health can have several degrees of worry. Say they have a broken leg. If the doctor says, "We can't do anything to fix it, the conditions are wrong," they suffer a lot. If the doctor says, "We can fix it, you can walk in 6 weeks," we feel a lot less pain. Either way, the essential pain is the same. It is our outlook that changes.

So, part of acceptance is the removal of the second arrow, the suffering that comes with self-criticism and negative outlook.

Suffering also carries with it an implication that we must do something about it. We live in a society that wants pain to be gone, be it physical or emotional. We try really hard to make suffering go away. With acceptance we may find ourselves realizing that we have tried all the ways we know to make the situation better, and that still we suffer. With this realization can come a re-assessment of the situation, and perhaps the feeling that, "It's already here, I guess I'll just have to feel it," and move on. Acceptance can work like that.

With mindfulness we have been exploring a different way, a way of allowing suffering to be in awareness. We have been realizing that pushing feelings away doesn't work, and is costly to us because it can shut parts of us down, and can actually cause increased mental stress. Allowing suffering to be felt may take a short or a long time. One thing we are working towards with the allowing is that our level of tolerance for the suffering increases. At some point, we may notice that our tolerance increased enough that we can bear the pain. This is a moment ripe for acceptance, the idea that now we could live with what we have.

With acceptance we may experience a sense of letting go, of yielding on our desire to control things, to fix things. This letting go can be quite a relief. We have been holding tight to the conviction that we can change the problem, must change the

problem....And one day we realize that is not working. We have
encountered acceptance.

There is also some sense that we are more grounded in reality
with acceptance, that we have looked clearly, a benefit of all that
allowing, have clearly seen the situation, opened our perspective,
and that we cannot change it any more than we have. This has a
similar sense to the Serenity Prayer used in 12-Step programs: God
grant me the serenity to accept the things I cannot change; courage
to change the things I can; and wisdom to know the difference.
The 12-Step programs often cite the words: Awareness, Acceptance,
Action, carrying the idea that after there is awareness, before we
take action we need to have acceptance. In that sense acceptance
also means going through a process of allowing, sitting with, seeing
clearly....All that before taking any sort of action, so that the
action may be helpful and not destructive.

Still, after we reach acceptance, some possibility of change may
yet appear. Perhaps a new medication for sleeplessness, or a cure for
allergies or the common cold. Perhaps I might go on some sort of
retreat that would radically change my spiritual life. Any of that is
still possible after reaching acceptance. The important part is that
I realize I have done what I can, that I have developed as much
tolerance as I reasonably can, and I come to the idea that I can live
with this difficulty.

With acceptance we may feel huge relief. The battle is over. We
have not won, but we have done what we can. We give up the
fight. Now our energy is freed up for other things, it is not caught
in some fight for survival. It is not consumed in a fight that is not
going anywhere. We are not living a fantasy that we will be the
gods who change the powers that be.

Life flows around us. We are carried along by forces in our family,
our town, our culture, our world. These forces are quite strong.
We are a few among many, many people. Some things we fight to
change. Others are just too big for us, so we learn we need to pick
our battles. There is a place for acceptance here.

The impact of this acceptance should not be underestimated. Anything that moves us from hopeless is powerful. While this idea is strong medicine and needs to be discussed gently with clients, it can be freeing.

Up Against the Current

We might feel that we were swimming in a cold river, against the current. We kept swimming, we felt that we had to avoid being swept up by the current. At some point awareness came, and we stopped, we just let ourselves float with the current. As we floated we felt the cold water around us, did not struggle against it. We allowed our experience to be. We got used to the feel of the water. It wasn't as bad as we thought. We could live with it. We had a degree of acceptance. We looked around. Without losing all our energy in the struggle to fight the current, we had energy left to consider our situation. What should we do now? Swim with the current?

Swimming with the current is like working with the world as it is. For example, if I felt that eating chickens just had to stop, because billions of animals are tortured and killed each year and that is untenable (and I do feel that) I might live with a sense of doom, because the problem is so much bigger than me. The doom would increase as I spoke to my friends about this, got nods, but not changes in behavior. And my despair might increase further at moments when I myself consumed chicken because of some circumstances. All of that has a sense of swimming against the current, because there are very powerful counter-forces pushing the opposite way to my desired direction.

At some moment I pause, assess the situation. That is like stopping the swimming and just floating for a while. I realize that I can't change the world, but maybe I can do a better job with my friends and myself, for example. At that point I have acceptance, the feeling that I can live with this difficulty. It is important to note that acceptance does not mean giving up. It does mean seeing clearly so that I can clearly discern what actions I might take.

Case Example:

Abdul

Abdul worked in a professional pressure cooker, he had to get things done on time, and his boss was exceedingly demanding. His boss would yell at him for what seemed like endless amounts of time. As Abdul listened he felt his self-confidence fading away, felt he could not survive these barrages of demands and criticism. He also felt anger rising up, but did not act on it, he needed the job. The anger made it harder to hear what was being said, and he made errors. He became aware that something needed to change.

Abdul took the Mindfulness-Based Cognitive Therapy workshop. He learned the principles outlined in this manual. He allowed the feelings of humiliation and anger to be in him, felt them in his heart and body. After some time with this he began to have some clarity, to see more clearly the situation. His boss was a troubled person. Perhaps he could change his boss, a long shot. Or perhaps he could change himself in some way. He had a better shot at that. He would try to live with this somehow.

He tried mindful listening, in which he listened just to hear his boss, not trying to analyze what he should do as he listened, just listening, and letting his boss know he was being heard. We can imagine that his boss might have realized something was different from a change in body language by Abdul. At any rate, his boss did not change his behavior.

Abdul experienced the yelling with a sense of peace when he didn't fight it in his head and heart, but rather just let it flow into him and around him. He became even more convinced he could live with this. When his boss was finished he would say thank you, and go to work on the project. Everything had changed in Abdul's experience, and yet nothing had changed in the outward manifestation of what was happening.

Jessica

Jessica was a recent college graduate with an internship at a major department store. Her work required her to make displays as needed, when requested. She could not control her work schedule. She could not control when she had coffee or bathroom brakes, either. Jessica had a urinary tract infection that for some time disrupted her bladder control. During that time period she lived in panic that she would wet her pants and embarrass herself. Now that problem was long gone, but she retained the fears. She often felt she had to urinate, and was never sure when the sensations were accurate, when fueled by worry.

In our treatment we worked with diet and liquid intake, and with allowing her fears to be present. Gradual exposure helped her live more easily with her fears, but there was a residual discomfort and fear. One day in treatment we decided to do an experiment. She would actually intensify the feared sensations, leaning forward in her chair in my office, causing pressure on her bladder to increase. We would observe the results. She did this, and reported the sensations increased, but she could bear them. Now, looking back, I remember we worked in this way for a few more sessions, and then stopped because her worry, and the related sensations, were no longer a problem. I realized that when she agreed to bend forward and increase the bladder pressure, she was essentially agreeing that she could live with the sensations, was moving into acceptance of her situation. With this way of understanding, the reason for her moving on from this difficulty is clear.

Betsy

Betsy is a married mother of two young children. At night she makes a plan for the next morning, so that she gets everything done in the morning. Get the kids up, dress them, feed them, make their lunch, talk with them, plus do all she needed for herself, and anticipate any needs of her husband. She took time before going to bed to plan all this out because she wanted the mornings to go smoothly, without pressure or raised voices. This was her goal, but despite her planning the mornings generally were chaotic. But she kept trying, day after day. Not surprisingly, each morning and evening she felt extreme self-blame for her poor performance. She kept trying, harder and harder, with not much change in the results.

We explored this in session. She had an epiphany: she could live with the chaos in the mornings. She would make an effort to organize, but however it came out was beyond her control. She had found acceptance of the situation. Her frustrations around this melted away.

Andrew

Andrew is studying improvisational comedy. He needs to be funny, but he can't use rehearsed jokes, the humor has to come out of his spontaneous responses to material from other actors or from the audience. He came to me knowing my specialty in mindfulness and psychotherapy, feeling that this mindfulness, awareness of the moment, might be helpful for his improv work.

The first thing we encountered was his judgmental voice. After his student performances he would tear himself apart with self-criticism. Awareness wasn't much of a problem for him, so we went right to working with his feelings after performance, and during the session as we explored it. First, during session, Andrew practiced noticing the feelings he had while discussing his performances with me, and allowing his feelings to be held in awareness. We often would pause during session to let the feelings be, noticing both the feelings and what was happening in his body. He practiced noticing his feelings before performance, and sitting with them, and also his feelings after, sitting with those. It was the feelings after performance that were particularly hard. He often used the 3-Minute Breathing Space as a way of taking good care of himself when the feelings became intense.

At the same time he learned basic breath meditation. In session we worked with the critical voice that told him he could never meditate, he would never get it right. Usually these thoughts came up when his mind wandered frequently from his intended focus on the breath. Our work was clear: if he could learn self-compassion for his wandering mind during breath meditation, perhaps that would carry over to his self-judgment after performances. Gradually he learned compassion for his wandering mind. He learned to treat each moment he realized he had been distracted as a happy moment, because he had just remembered his intention. In the old way, each time he remembered would be a moment of self-hatred, with thoughts like, "There you go again, you're such a loser."

Over time Andrew did learn these things, consistent with the idea that for many people when compassion is alive in them, it goes across different activities, and even gets applied to other people. Finally, one day Andrew told me he had accepted that improv is essentially imperfect, he would live with this reality.

Mary

Mary was accomplished in sales. She presented to clients, and they bought her services. She came to me when she wanted to present to groups of people who might benefit from her skills.

She felt too nervous to carry this out, even though her professional credentials were very strong. She had thoughts that she wouldn't be a good enough speaker, wouldn't be able to organize group presentations well enough that they would hold attention, and that her ideas would not stand out as special. We explored her history with speaking in public. In college she had gathered her courage and auditioned for a part in a play, and won it. She burst into tears as she remembered this success. She began to talk about why she felt this was so emotional for her. I asked her if we could pause, so she could really experience her feelings. She agreed. She sat with her feelings, noticed thoughts coming up (a few of which we talked about), felt a variety of feelings and body sensations. At the end of the session she was sure: she would give the talks a try. She couldn't guarantee the results, but she would live with them.

What is the Flavor of Accepting?

Imagine that we have a tangle of fishing line, or thread, and we need to get it untangled right away. If we don't, something bad will happen. We pull here, we pull there, loosen here, loosen there, and it just seems to be getting worse. We try harder and harder to no avail.

So we stop, we pause. We take a breath, noticing our feelings for a few moments. Our heart is pounding. We are in a pickle, with little time to do a difficult task. We realize we were caught in a rush of actions, hoping for the best. We look closely at the tangle, seeing some details. We see the complexity of it. Now we have some idea of the nature of this tangle, and see some possible approaches we might try within the time available.

This is what accepting can look like. It can come quickly, as in this case. Before acceptance we are caught in a rush of actions, after accepting we are able to see things more clearly, and have a sense that we can handle the situation.

With these understandings, this quote from Carl Rogers may be better understood: "The curious paradox is that when I accept myself just as I am, then I can change." - from his book, *On Becoming A Person*. With acceptance, as I use the word, we free up the energy that went into trying to change things, we realize we have done what we can. Probably we realize that the struggling went on much longer than it needed to, longer than it was productive. With this can come a sort of relaxation, because we are not struggling against a huge force. This energy is now available for other things. In this sense, we can more easily change after we have accepted ourselves, because we no longer carry the feeling of fighting against something impossible. Now we are free, we can see clearly, we can work on changing ourselves in ways that are possible.

Acceptance in action

Victor Frankl was a Jew in a Nazi concentration camp. He and the others there lived in rags, with only tiny morsels of food to eat. They were skin and bones. Yet he went around to people trying to cheer them up, sharing his food with them. This was acceptance in action. Later he wrote, in <u>Man's Search for Meaning</u>, "Everything can be taken from a man but one thing: the last of the human freedoms - to choose one's attitude in any given set of circumstances, to choose one's own way."

A Therapeutic Choice

With these concepts we realize a therapeutic choice.

> We can
> -work with the situation at hand, or we can
> -accept it and move on.

For a therapist and client to entertain the possibility of acceptance we need to look closely at efforts made so far, need to have confidence that they have been sufficient, and that other alternatives for change have not been overlooked. Only then might we suggest an exploration of acceptance of the issue at hand.

A Case Conceptualization involving Acceptance

At intake Frank revealed a lifetime of ADD and a goal to gain control over these unwanted thoughts through mindfulness meditation. He had tried psychotropic medication for the ADD, but did not like the side-effects. He had tried to quiet his mind on his own by living in a spiritual, meditative community, but that did not help. He had tried meditating 45 minutes a day, and that did not quiet his thoughts.

Frank's wish is to learn to quiet his mind. I explained that my work would not likely help with that, but could rather help him accept his active, inattentive mind. He had told me he is quite successful at his work, and maintains an intimate relationship. Since his functioning was high (the ADD was not inhibiting his career or personal life), I explained, acceptance seemed like a possible goal.

He immediately felt sadness at this prospect, sadness that he would not be able to gain control of his mind. I felt sadness also, that he had spent years trying to change his essential self in order to avoid feeling the sadness.

I then introduced him to the concept of emotional avoidance, explaining that we sometimes put a lot of energy into not feeling emotions, because they are too painful or uncomfortable. It seemed to me that he was avoiding feeling sadness over the nature of his mind, his ADD, by focusing for years and years on finding a way to change his mind, to quiet it.

I explained some of the research on experiential avoidance, the energy it takes, the way it can lead to bottled emotions that actually gain in strength, whereas taking the opposite approach of letting the emotions be felt in his body helps them flow through. I explained that it can be very helpful to learn to tolerate and even allow the feelings, let them flow through him and pass away like waves, and that mindfulness teaches this.

I felt that his time in a meditative community may not have helped because the object of meditation is to focus on one thing, usually the breath. A tough order for someone with ADD. Perhaps concentration had been emphasized at the expense of self-acceptance. While most teachers say to return without judgment, the degree of emphasis on this is typically much stronger in a mental health environment.

At this moment Frank remembered that when in college he had broken down in tears once, and sobbed, and how cathartic it was... But that hadn't lasted, his ongoing sadness and self-criticism just returned after awhile. I explained that this method of letting the emotions pass through is not a miracle cure, but a gradual letting go, with a general change over time. We are not promising miracle cures, but rather a different way of relating to experience, with allowing rather than pushing it away, so that we live with the flow of our emotions, learning we need not fear them, but can tolerate them and live more freely. We can learn to see emotions as waves that rise and fall.

Frank progressed rapidly towards acceptance, and moved on to other elements of his life.

Working Towards Acceptance

We and our clients may have moments of clarity, such as I did with my sleeplessness, or it may take a process to develop this acceptance. The moments of clarity can come at surprising moments, and we hope to be alert to them when they occur. Sometimes we are lucky! Our clients, however, may tend to get stuck and need to go through a process of acceptance.

The process to develop this acceptance needs to include gaining a sense of calm and perspective, as we can achieve with awareness and allowing. The allowing helps us learn to tolerate feelings so they are no longer avoided. When we can know all our experience we can see things clearly, can have deeper understanding. With this clarity we can begin to explore acceptance.

The bird in the sky

In a sense, it as if when we are stuck in a worry, our perspective becomes distorted as we focus on the problem. If we can visualize that worry as a bird, the bird is all we can see. After we have realized acceptance our perspective changes, and we can see that the bird is in a huge sky, where many possibilities for action exist.

The process must not end there. We are not resigned. Rather, we are seeing clearly. With that clarity we are ready to consider what actions we might take.

CHAPTER SIX

Acting: With Perspective, We Can Choose Actions Wisely

I was lost in sadness. My marriage had collapsed, both my parents had died, and my career was not going well. Every morning I sat quietly at home and let the feelings flow through me. Every morning I asked myself what I needed to do that day. Sometimes it came to me that I needed to smile at people. Other days that I needed to focus on work. Other days that I needed to eat better. I understood that my next actions were the most important ones I could take. I also thought about the future. Then it came to me: I could consider a new career, maybe become a minister, maybe a journalist, maybe a psychotherapist. I explored these for a year, then made my decision.

From the point of view of mindfulness, one action is the most important, and that is the very next action we take, since it is the only one we can definitely control. From the point of view of mindfulness, our life consists of a series of such actions.

We all get into times of bad choices, actions we regret, or even actions not taken that we regret. With mindfulness, we can always have the hope that we will realize we have been operating on automatic pilot, then remember mindfulness, regain our perspective, and get back on track with a helpful action.

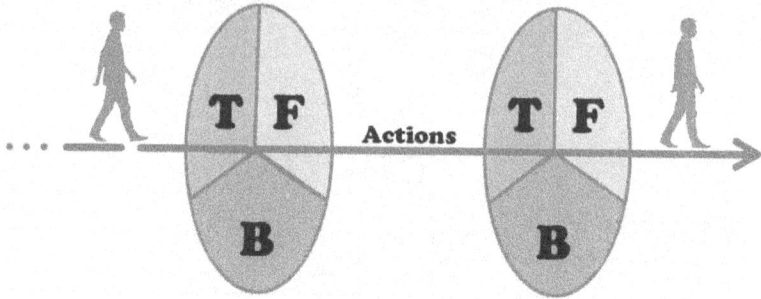

Illustration: Life is a series of moments, with inclinations to action

Awareness is made up of thoughts, feelings and body sensations. We can add that awareness also includes an inclination to action. These inclinations move us through life. Note: we use T for thoughts, F for feelings, and B for body.

Daily Activities

What better place to start looking at our actions than by considering the things we do every day? We can start by examining our usual daily actions. We may make a list of things we do each day, starting with getting up and ending with going to sleep. The list might begin:

Wake up
Wash
Dress
Eat breakfast
Check e-mail
Walk to the train
Arrive at work
Greet co-workers...

Then, we think about each item on our list, and mark it with a D if it depletes our energy, or with an N if it nourishes our energy. Now we have a chance to look at our day, a series of actions, and to understand where our energy is going. We may consider doing more of the nourishing activities or less of the depleting ones.

And there is yet another sort of action we can take: we can examine our attitude and acceptance towards the depleting ones, and see if it is possible to make a change there, not to fight the inevitable, but to do the task with curiosity rather than anger or anxiety.

Pleasure, Mastery and Generosity Actions

We can also look at additional activities that might be helpful, every day or in times of distress. At these times we may need to take extra good care of ourselves.

In thinking about helpful actions, we might remember that many choices are available. When feeling low we might habitually think of taking actions that give us pleasure, such as taking a shower, listening to music, seeing a friend, reading something pleasurable. That may well be exactly what we need. It can be helpful to make a list of pleasure actions, and plan some of them into our schedule. We can also refer to the list when we experience distress, and use them as a way to take good care of ourselves.

We may also realize that doing mastery activities, things that are productive, also can be helpful. This might include actions such as paying some bills, cooking some food, cleaning out a closet. The sense of accomplishment we get from these actions may help nurture a sense of efficacy, defeating thoughts of hopelessness. Even an action that puts a small doubt into the conviction of personal helplessness can be really helpful. It can be the beginning of rebuilding a sense of power in our own lives. As with pleasure activities, it can be helpful to schedule a few into our schedule, and keep a list handy.

In addition to considering actions that are directly helpful to ourselves, we can consider other-oriented actions. Research has found that we may actually get more emotional benefit from giving things away than from accumulating more for ourselves. It's worth thinking about this, or experimenting for ourselves.

Pleasurable activities – things we easily enjoy

Mastery activities – things that can give us a sense of accomplishment

Generosity activities – things that give us a sense of being worthy people

We may protest that we do not have the time to add more activities to our lives, we so busy already. Looking into this a bit can be helpful. We tend to put a lot of our time into essential activities that need to be done now. Work, for example, or parenting. We can get so exhausted doing those activities that when we get home we just crash, turn on the radio or tv, and zone out. When we are able to add in some balance to our lives, managing the work/parenting dynamic, or other time demands, we may feel less depleted and less needy of crash time. That can free up the energy needed to do things that strengthen us, such as the exercises in this manual, and the nourishing activities we have been exploring. For a more detailed description of this approach of using our time, please see the book 7 *Habits of Highly Effective People.*

Actions, When We Have a Level of Upset

It may be that we still find that emotions come on strong as we approach the idea of action. When this happens we can do some more work with feelings and thoughts.

This takes us back to the 3-Minute Breathing Space. We discussed a breathing space for regular use, and another for coping. At the end of the 3-Minute Breathing Space – Coping we focused on our body, noticing areas of discomfort or distress, and practiced allowing our attention to focus down into just those parts of our body where distress was strongest.

Now we can take that a step further. Besides noticing our body and distress in it, we can notice feelings and thoughts, and consider what actions we might take.

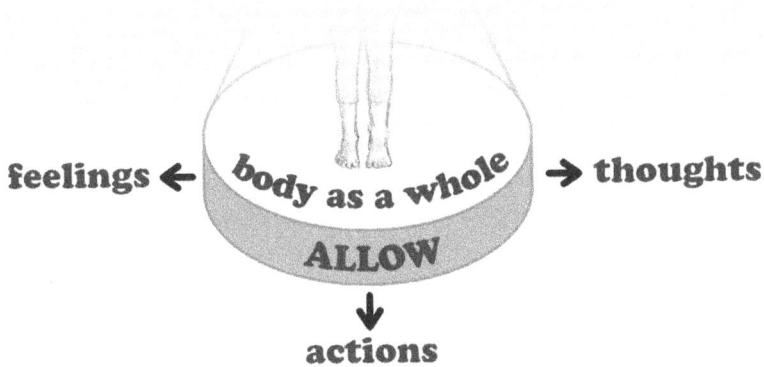

feelings ← body as a whole → thoughts

ALLOW

↓

actions

Illustration: After the 3-Minute Breathing Space, we have choices

What might we do next? We might simply return to the activities of our day, or we might work with our feelings, or we might work with our thoughts, or we might take some skillful action.

Working with Feelings

When feelings are strong in us, strong enough that we lose the energy needed to move forward, we may want to pause and allow them to be present, taking good care of ourselves in the process, and allowing the feelings to flow through us. So, after the 3-Minute Breathing Space – Coping, we check our feelings, monitor their nature and intensity. Are they feelings of sadness, anger, anxiety, grief, frustration? Are they so strong that we are close to panic, or are they tolerably strong, or barely upsetting? If they are too strong, we use the methods described in the chapter on allowing to take good care of ourselves. If they are strong but bearable then we sit with them, drawing our attention away from the combination of thoughts and feelings that can be so toxic, and towards the combination of feelings and body that can be really grounding. We allow the feelings and body sensations to be the focus of our attention for as long as is needed. If they continue on at a level of strength that warrants it, we do the Working with Difficulty practices.

Working with Thoughts

When negative thoughts are strong in us, strong enough that we realize we are not thinking clearly, we may want to pause and allow them to be present, taking good care of ourselves in the process. We practice seeing them as events in the mind rather than as concrete manifestations of reality. We may examine the evidence for and against their truthfulness. We may write them down, taking away their vague sense of reality. We can do this in the time immediately after taking a 3-Minute Breathing Space – Coping, and if this is not enough we can go back to the chapter on allowing, and do the Working with Thoughts practices. We also can use Working with Difficulty.

Working with Actions

We may take some actions which are new to us, after we have worked with this material for awhile.

What then?

We can think of this process as a loop: after the action we return to the process of mindfulness. So, we take a new action. We intend to have awareness as we do it. We take some time to breathe or center ourselves before we take it, so we can awaken from automatic pilot, and be aware of ourselves as we take the action. As we take it, we slow down, the better to notice our internal experience of thoughts, feelings and body sensations. We bring curiosity to the action – who knows what we will discover! Perhaps we follow our breath as an anchor to stay in the present. Then, after we have taken the action, we pause and watch the flow of our experience for awhile, not jumping quickly into the next actions of our day.

In this way we have a lot of information about our experience of the action, and a chance to understand ourselves more deeply. After that we may even decide to sit with the memory of the experience, to know it even more deeply.

Working with Long-term Decisions

We may be wondering if we should deepen a relationship, or take a new job, or do something entirely new. In these cases a lot of information and understanding is needed. We do not decide to live with an elephant with a blindfold on (without awareness) and with only touching it in one place. We would be deciding how to relate to a tail, or a leg, or a trunk! Instead we need to touch the elephant in many places before we can understand it.

So we sit down many times, noticing our thoughts, our feelings, and our bodies. We sit and wait for insight many, many times. We sit, and each time we find some answers about what we need to do now, and some kernels of truth about our future. And each time we gain in understanding, moving towards a moment that we can know what our longer-term decision must be.

We will need information from the outside world too, of course. We need to know the river we are swimming in.

In the case of bigger actions, with more long-term impact, we gather a lot of information, over a long period of time, so that one fine day we have a moment of knowing our direction. We slow down. We stay aware. We pay a lot of attention to our experience. We allow our feelings to flow through us. We find times of acceptance. We act. We always act, it is just that some actions have short-term consequences, some long-term.

What's My Next Right Action?

The actions we take in life determine our legacy.

So we develop a habit of asking ourselves , "What's my next right action?" We use the word right not in a moral sense but rather in the sense that it is a response more than a reaction, that it is wise in the sense of being helpful for us and others, that it is…. Right.

CHAPTER SEVEN

After Practicing in the Present

There are some pleasant side effects and insights from these practices of awareness, allowing, acceptance and action.

Happiness

There is research indicating that much of our happiness is genetically determined (by a sort of set point), that a small part is determined by circumstances (the size of our apartment, for example) and that another big part is determined by our intentional activities (things we choose to do.) (See Ed Diener and Richard Davidson's research, for example.)

The part of our happiness that is determined by circumstances needs no discussion here. It is the topic of large swaths of cultural and educational learning and understanding. However, understanding that it isn't the major factor in feeling happy frees us to spend less time changing these circumstances. Less **emphasis** on getting the right apartment, car, job, partner. And that frees us up to spend more time on the other factors.

The part of our happiness that is determined by our intentional activities is very much the topic of this manual. Awareness, allowing, acceptance, all help guide us towards actions that are wise, considered, non-reactive, helpful. That has had particular emphasis in the last chapter.

The part that is genetically influenced is of great interest in the context of this manual.

Thinking about acceptance and change, if we can bring acceptance to the genetically influenced parts, just letting them be as described in the chapter on acceptance, then we can relate to our experience in a wholly different way than if we were cursing our genetic heritage. Just think of accepting the rain that is about to soak us, and applying that to a lifetime. Or accepting that we have a quirky sort of intelligence, or that we have ADD, or inadequate education, or just one leg.

When we fight against the set-point of our happiness, the day-to-day portion of happiness that seems to be a norm, we may live lives of discontent. When we can accept that set-point, making the most of things anyway, we can experience a very different way of being in life.

Overall then, we might find that awareness, allowing, acceptance and actions can go a long way towards enabling happiness.

9 Verbs of Mindfulness

We can begin to understand mindfulness as a state of mind, and a process of actions.

1. Pause, slow down for a moment, notice what's present: your senses (sounds, sights, smells, textures, tastes), as well as thoughts, emotions, and body sensations.

2. Welcome what you notice. It may be nice, it may be messy, but welcome it all with an attitude of curiosity. It may be getting you ready for something special.

3. Experience what you notice, staying with it, whether it's pleasant, unpleasant, or confusing.

4. Allow your experience to continue in your awareness, even if it keeps evolving.

5. Feel your emotions, remembering that there are no wrong emotions, only wrong actions.

6. Suffer, allow your feelings to be in you (using your good judgment), remembering feelings are like waves even though they trick you into feeling they're forever.

7. Move your awareness to your body. It is a great place to feel your emotions, taking you away from the thoughts that create a feedback-loop, locking emotions in. Feeling emotions in your body allows them to exist, then to flow through you, and out of you.

8. Be present with what you notice, allowing yourself to be curious about the smallest, seemingly insignificant parts of your experience.

9. Act wisely, something that will be easier now, with your mind calmer. Your actions matter, and in particular your next action matters. You may choose something profound, or something immediate, that's up to you. But choose your next action wisely! Who knows what course it will set you on.

The 14 Facts of Mindfulness

There are a few facts that sum up the principles of mindfulness in psychotherapy.

1. The present matters.

2. We are usually on automatic pilot.

3. Experiential avoidance is a problem.

4. Meditation means focusing on one thing, like the breath.

5. Mindfulness means noticing the present, without judgment.

6. We can connect to the present by noticing body sensations, emotions, thoughts, inclinations towards action, or the 5 senses.

7. Mindfulness is learned experientially.

8. Right away we notice how easily our attention is distracted, and we begin to practice accepting this self that has a mind that wanders.

9. Mindfulness means allowing all of our experience to be just as it is, in the moment, without chasing it away, allowing the parts we like, and allowing the parts we don't like.

10. We increase the depth of our encounter with life by learning to allow negative experience, then to stay with it, then to introduce it into our awareness on purpose, then learning to ride the waves of emotion as they move through us.

11. We find that emotions can be felt through our bodies, that this is more easily tolerated than staying in the feedback loop of thoughts and emotions.

12. We find that we are better at choosing helpful actions when we have cultivated mindfulness.

13. We enrich our relationships through compassion and mindful listening and speaking.

14. We realize that there are two fundamental ways of 'being': lost in the mind, or mindful of the present.

The Promises of Engaged Mindfulness

Amid all the writing on this subject, it is easy to lose focus on the prize. We can expect:

1. **The ability to drop into the present**, a time when there is more right than wrong. Many worries relate to the future, many regrets relate to the past.

2. **A reservoir of self-esteem** that comes from encountering our actual self again and again in the present. It's not that we 'improve' in order to deserve this self-esteem, but rather that we grow to appreciate and accept this me who 'is' ... Even while we are on a path towards 'becoming.'

3. **Skills allowing us to relate differently** to our negative thoughts and emotions, so they have less power over us, so they don't pull us away from our desired focus – whether that focus is a loved-one, work, nature, a project, or a contemplation.

4. **Compassion for ourselves and others**, arising out of our more accurate perceptions of ourselves and our world.

5. **Choice in where we focus your attention**, and choice in the options for wise action that we perceive.

6. **Perspective on problems**, the ability to see the whole picture, to see clearly, prerequisites to wise actions.

7. **Wisdom to take actions that are right for us**... Be they large or small. We will find that when we connect to our experience in the present we can see things clearly and choose our next actions wisely.

Summary

Some of us find life stressful and get into patterns of automatically going about our tasks day to day. Life becomes boring. Curiosity takes a nap. We are on automatic pilot.

At some point, we awake to the reality of how we are living. We wonder if there is a better way. We become aware of birdsong, of the sky, of our sensing bodies, of our feelings. We even gain enough perspective to watch our own thinking process and realize how frivolous it is, and how controlling it is. Our thoughts affect our moods. Our moods affect our thoughts. So we continue to progress, to find refuge in our bodies. We feel in our bodies. We satisfy our curiosity with body awareness. We are aware.

We realize that this awareness extends to wonderful experiences, and to unpleasant ones. We realize we cannot just notice the banana, we must also notice the peel. We begin to understand the high cost of aversion, of trying to live with rose-colored glasses. So we begin to experiment with allowing all this awareness to be present, to stay in us, and eventually we become able to sit with all this, as we allow it to be in awareness.

Still, we have some dissatisfaction with the way things are. There are lots of things we don't like, some we like. It seems like this liking-not-liking extends to just about everything, excepting those things that so overwhelm us that we banish them from awareness. Gradually we find out that we can accept the things that we don't like, as unpleasant as they may be.

Then, one fine day, after integrating mindfulness into our lives, we become so enchanted with life around us that we feel a lightness in our chest, and realize that we have choices. Not the sort of choices that rock the earth, but moment-by-moment choices of what individual actions we will take, and we find out from experience that choosing those actions wisely really makes a difference in the lives we lead. We are more free than we ever imagined.

1. Aware, we work in the present

2. Allowing, we work with the pleasant, the unpleasant, and the confusing

3. Accepting, we immerse ourselves in what is, opening ourselves to growth

4. Acting, we regain perspective and choose wise, helpful actions.

About the Author
and Acknowledgments

Remember the story of the 3 blind men and the elephant? They were asked to describe it. The first blind man reached out and touched something long, like a snake, but with a lot of hair at the end. "It's like a snake with a hairy mouth," he taught. The second blind man reached out and felt the elephant's leg. "It's like a tree with soft bark and prickles like a cactus," he opined. The third blind man reached out and felt something long and wrinkly, hanging down, with hot air coming out of it.... then this big sucking sound... as it sucked the peanut right out of his hand! "It's like nothing I've ever experienced. It breathes out hot air, and when it breathes in it creates a

Donald Fleck

giant suction. It took my peanut and left my hand all wet. Then it stroked my cheek in the most tender way. It's both scary and tender, breathes in and breathes out." In such a way people can examine one thing and see it in many different ways.

It's the same with mindfulness. The way it's described depends on where you touch it. There's Mahayana and Theraveda, Vipassana and Zen, medical and religious and spiritual. Eastern and Western. This mindfulness of this teacher or that teacher. And it really matters which one you learn from. Not that one is clearly better than another, but that each has its own special advantages.

My first contact with mindfulness came of necessity. I was working on Wall Street, helping manage the Merrill Lynch advertising campaign, "Bullish on America." The job was really stressful. We were expected to make really effective ads and at the same time satisfy all sorts of lawyers and regulatory agencies. Add to that deadlines we could not miss. I was stressed out of my mind. I saw a book, *The Relaxation Response* by Herbert Benson, and read it. He said I could find calm by noticing my breathing and saying over and over again, "One, one, one..." I walked a few blocks up Broadway to a quiet place, sat there - usually all by myself-breathing in ("one"), out ("one"), in ("one"), out ("one"). It helped, a lot. I'd go back to work and power through the rest of the day. Benson made the point that we didn't have to learn a new religion to get the benefits of meditation, we could take out that part and the rest would be enough. (Years later he wrote another book describing a more spiritual approach, and that also helped many people.)

I have appreciated the reporting of Bill Moyers for many years. He is a wise teacher. His interview of Joseph Campbell in which Campbell says, "Eternity exists, in this moment," gave me the understanding I might have gotten from a 500 page book. What a clarifying thought! Also powerful was his series Medicine and the Mind. In that one he had a segment on Jon Kabat-Zinn and Mindfulness-Based Stress Reduction, developed at Mass Medical Center. He taught mindfulness to everyday people: truck drivers, health care workers, housewives, not your run-of-the mill mindfulness candidates. He made mindfulness available to everyone with an 8-week workshop designed for folks with untreatable pain. Later the workshop was extended to people with stress and other ailments. Seeing that show was like an out-of-body experience. I was inspired, shocked, hopeful. The words and images remain in the fibers of my body. Wow! Mindfulness in medicine.

A few years after that my marriage ended, and my Dad died, then my Mom died. I was 45. I was hit in my face by 3 bolts of lightening in rapid succession, and decided it was time to leave behind marketing and try something new. I looked into the ministry, journalism, and psychotherapy. To try out the ministry I started giving homilies and sermons at my Unitarian Church. My friend Charlotte and I decided to do one on meditation. How could we teach meditation to a church congregation? Have 15 minutes of silence? That didn't seem like it could work! When we met to figure out how to give the sermon I pulled out a copy of Thich Nhat Hanh's *Blooming of a Lotus*, a series of guided meditations I had found in my local bookstore. She pulled out the same book! Thay (as Thich Nhat Hanh is often called by his students) is an amazing teacher. The sermon went well. The church started a weekly meditation group that continued for years. And I began exploring the teachings of this wise man in depth. They have greatly influenced how I approach mindfulness in psychotherapy.

After the 3 losses I started long-term treatment with a psychotherapist. She thought I should become a therapist myself, and predicted I would use mindfulness meditation in my work. At the time I was using a method of consciously bringing to mind the 3 tragedies each morning, and sitting with the feelings that came up. It sort of grew out of my improvised meditation practice, those "one's" as I breathed with awareness on Wall Street. I'd sit with the feelings until I got a clear idea of what I was supposed to do that day. Each day I waited for wise guidance. It did not matter to me if the guidance was coming from a spirit larger than myself, or from my unconscious, or from my calm mind. I'd just wait. The guidance that came to me included things like, "Go out and smile," or "Do a good deed for someone," or "Take care of your self today," or "Buy some french fries." Which is sort of a long way of saying I was using meditation to feel and heal. Becoming a psychotherapist became the obvious choice.

After completing my study of clinical social work, I started my dozen years at the Jewish Board. Soon after starting there I bought a copy of *Full Catastrophe Living*, by Jon Kabat Zinn, describing his 8-week program. I began trying out some of his teachings with my clients. It was clear that using the breath to calm and see clearly was helpful. I taught this to a few people, and it worked until they came back and said it hadn't worked one time, so they were abandoning it. I had not understood that meditation can be helpful, but can't be used like a pill. Using it like aspirin to remove a headache wouldn't work. I had to understand it more deeply, so enrolled in a course on Vipassana mediation at New York's Open Center. There followed many other trainings, over many years. I had a weekend training with Jack Kornfield. He gave me a deeper understanding, and the knowledge that meditation teachers can have a light touch, be funny and enlightened. His book *A Path With Heart* was especially helpful. Soon after I came across Tara Brach's book *Radical Acceptance*. Written for the layperson, I realized that if I read her case examples carefully I could piece together a method for using mindfulness in psychotherapy. I did it just as Jung had to piece together Freud's method from a vague paragraph in a professional journal, when he first encountered Freud's then-new psychoanalysis. Tara Brach's book took me far.

Then I met Mary Myers, who was advancing her work as a healer, and I offered to help her build her practice. We started talking, and it turned out she wanted to use something called Mindfulness-Based Cognitive Therapy (MBCT). It grew out of Mindfulness-Based Stress Reduction, but is designed for use in mental health. I also had read about MBCT, but felt it was too daunting to learn on my own. And now: here was this other teacher interested in the same thing! So we decided to teach a group together, we helped each other. It worked wonderfully. Sadly, we could not afford to teach together after that, so went our own ways. That first workshop was 8 years ago, 27 groups ago, 250 people ago. MBCT has proven to be the biggest contributor to my use of mindfulness in psychotherapy. Each time I offer the workshop I teach it a little bit differently. This keeps it fresh for the participants, and helps me try out new things. I took the 5-day residential training at Omega Institute, taught by MBCT co-author Zindel Segal and his associate Susan Woods. Later I took another 5-day residential on the ways of engaging clients in discovery learning in mindfulness-based approaches. And I learned mindfulness-based-work experientially by taking Mindfulness-Based Stress Reduction with Elaine Retholtz in New York City.

I must not neglect the workshop participants. Each one of them has taught me something, and there have been 300. In particular, when I started drawing little pictures to illustrate key concepts there were calls for more – thanks for that, guys! And there was a day one participant asked me if maybe thinking was a defense. Each in their own way, all 250 have contributed to the understandings in this manual.

I also thank my individual psychotherapy clients, who taught me so much as I applied these lessons and adapted them for individual psychotherapy.

Many books have proven helpful. Most recently *The Wise Heart* by Jack Kornfield has provided gems of insight. Even his few pages on the three Buddhist personality types helped me understand the fundamentals, along with his discussion of the idea that each person has a personality that can be used well, or used badly. It's not that people are sick or healthy, he explained, but more like they are using 'who they are' well or poorly. What an insight! Psychotherapists do not always 'heal'. Rather, sometimes we teach people to accept who they are, and work with it.

I apologize to all the teachers I have left out. My wife, my children, my friends, my men's group, my collegial support group, my therapist teaching group, my meditation group, the many people who have attended my Days of Mindfulness at the public library. For the past 8 years mindfulness has been central to both my professional and my personal life.

Above all, my focus for the past 8 years has been on teaching Mindfulness-Based Cognitive Therapy (MBCT) in groups, and in using mindfulness in individual sessions with clients. The teachings of MBCT are so profound, they have influenced every element of this manual. In a way, it is simply an adaptation of MBCT to work with individuals with a wide variety of needs. Thank you Zindel Segal, Mark Williams and Jon Teasdale for creating this important treatment, and then for shepherding it through trials, and for enriching the process with your revised text ten years later. Thanks in particular to Zindel Segal, who taught me and so many others in North America how to facilitate MBCT groups. MBCT is now one of those rare powerful and empirically-based treatments, and provides the foundation on which a range of mindfully-based treatments are being developed.

Books and articles referenced in this manual

Foundational Books

Segal, Zindel; Williams, Mark; Teasdale, John; <u>Mindfulness-Based Cognitive Therapy for Depression</u>, Second Edition, Guilford Press, 2013
For therapists who want to know the details of MBCT as well as the research basis and history.

Williams, Mark; Teasdale, John; Zindel Segal; <u>The Mindful Way Through Depression</u>, Guildford, 2007
For clients and therapists, a lay explanation of MBCT.

Teasdale, John; Williams, Mark; Segal, Zindel; <u>The Mindful Way Workbook</u>, Guilford, 2014
For clients primarily (also useful for therapists), a supplement for what we teach our clients in session.

Kornfield, Jack, <u>The Wise Heart, A Guide to the Universal Teachings of Buddhist Psychology</u>, Bantam edition, 2009
For therapists, a text that deepens understanding and provides new concepts for research.

Books and articles referred to in the manual

Benson, Herbert, <u>the Relaxation Response</u>, Harper Torch edition, 2000

Brach, Tara, <u>Radical Acceptance: Embracing Your Life With the Heart of a Buddha</u>, Bantam edition, 2004

Covey, Stephen, The 7 Habits of Highly Effective People: Powerful Lessons in Personal Change, Simon & Schuster edition, 2013

Davidson, Richard, Buddha's Brain: The Practical Neuroscience of Happiness, Love, and Wisdom, New Harbinger Publications, 2009

Diener, Ed, Happiness: Unlocking the Mysteries of Psychological Wealth, Wiley-Blackwell, 2008

Frederickson, Barbara, Love 2.0, Creating Happiness and Health in Moments of Connection, Plume edition, 2013

Kabat-Zinn, Jon, Full Catastrophe Living: Using the Wisdom of Your Body and Mind to Face Stress, Pain, and Illness, Bantam edition, 2013

Kornfield, Jack, A Path With Heart: A Guide Through the Perils and Promises of Spiritual Life, Bantam edition, 1993

Miller, Alice, The Drama of the Gifted Child, The Search for the True Self, Basic Books Edition, 1997

Moyers, Bill, and Campbell, Joseph, The Power of Myth, Anchor Books edition, 1991

Moyers, Bill, Healing and the Mind, Public Broadcasting System, 1995

Nhat Hanh, Thich, Blooming of a Lotus, Beacon Press edition, 2009

Ouspensky, PD, The Psychology of Man's Possible Evolution, Vintage Books edition, 1973

Rogers, Carl, On Becoming a Person: A Therapist's View of Psychotherapy, Constable and Robinson edition, 2004

Articles

Dunn, Elizabeth; Aknin, Lara; Norton, Michael; Prosocial Spending and Happiness: Using Money to Benefit Others Pays Off, in Current Directions in Psychological Science, Volume 23, 2014

Dunn, Elizabeth; Aknin, Lara; Norton, Michael; Spending Money on Others Promotes Happiness, Science, 21 March 2008

Hayes, Steven, Experiential Avoidance and Behavioral Disorders: A functional dimensional approach to diagnosis and treatment, in the Journal of Consulting and Clinical Psychology, December 1996

Friedman, R and Forster J, The effects of Promotion and Prevention Cues on Creativity, Journal of Personality and Social Psychology, 2001, No. 6

For Further Study

Bartley, Trish, Mindfulness-Based Cognitive Therapy for Cancer, Wiley Blackwell, 2011

Bien, Thomas, Mindful Therapy: A Guide for Therapists and Helping Professionals, Wisdom Publications, 2006

Bowen, Sarah; Chawla, Neha; Mindfulness-Based Relapse Prevention for Addictive Behaviors: A Clinician's Guide, Guilford, 2010

Brach, Tara, True Refuge: Finding Peace and Freedom in Your Own Awakened Heart, Bantam, 2012

Brantley, Jeffrey, Calming Your Anxious Mind: How Mindfulness and Compassion Can Free You From Anxiety, Fear and Panic, New Harbinger, 2007

Carlson, Linda; Speca, Michael; Mindfulness-Based Cancer Recovery: A Step-by-Step MBSR Approach to Help You Cope with Treatment and Reclaim Your Life, New Harbinger, 2011

Crane, Rebecca; Mindfulness-Based Cognitive Therapy: Distinctive Features (CBT Distinctive Features), Routledge, 2008

Deckersbach, Thilo; Holzel, Britta; Eisner, Lori; Lazar, Sara; Nierenberg, Andres; Mindfulness-Based Cognitive Therapy for Bipolar Disorder, Guilford, 2014

Epstein, Mark, Psychotherapy Without the Self: a Buddhist Perspective, Yale University Press, 2007

Epstein, Mark, Going to Pieces Without Falling Apart: A Buddhist Perspective on Wholeness, Broadway Books, 1998

Epstein, Mark, The Trauma of Everyday Life, Penguin Press, 2013

Fortuna, Lisa; Vallejo, Zayda; Meleo-Meyer, Florence; Treating Co-occurring Adolescent PTSD and Addiction: Mindfulness-Based Cognitive Therapy for Adolescents with Trauma and Substance-Abuse Disorders, Context Press, 2015

Germer, Christopher; Siegel, Ronald; Fulton, Paul; Mindfulness and Psychotherapy, Second Edition, Guilford, 2013

Germer, Christopher; Siegel, Ronald; The Dalai Lama; Wisdom and Compassion in Psychotherapy: Deepening Mindfulness in Clinical Practice, Guilford Press, 2014

Gilbert, Daniel, Stumbling on Happiness, Vintage, 2006

Glasner-Edwards, The Addiction Recovery Skills Workbook: Changing Addictive Behaviors Using CBT, Mindfulness, and Motivational Interviewing Techniques, New Harbinger, 2015

Goldstein, Elisha, Uncovering Happiness: Overcoming Depression with Mindfulness and Self-Compassion , Atria Books, 2015

Hayes, Steven; Follette, Victoria; Linehan, Marsha; Mindfulness and Acceptance: Expanding the Cognitive-Behavioral Tradition, Guildford, 2004

Hershfield, Jon; Corboy, Tom; The Mindfulness Workbook for OCD: A Guide to Overcoming Obsessions and Compulsions Using Mindfulness and Cognitive Behavioral Therapy , New Harbinger, 2013

Kabat-Zinn, Jon, Wherever You Go There You Are: Mindfulness Meditation in Everyday Life, Hyperion edition, 2005

Nhat-Hanh, Thich, Buddhism and Psychotherapy (9 audio tapes), Parallax Press, 1989

McCown, Donald; Reibel, Diane; Micozzi, Marc; Teaching Mindfulness: A Practical Guide for Clinicians and Educators, Springer, 2010

Nhat-Hanh, Thich, The Practice of Mindfulness in Psychotherapy: (CD): Working with Anger and Nourishing Inner Peace Each and Every Day, Especially for Psychotherapists, Sounds True Recordings edition, 2006

Nhat Hanh, Thich, Reconciliation: Healing the Inner Child, Parallax Press, 2010

Orsillo, Susan; Roemer, Lizabeth; The Mindful Way through Anxiety: Break Free from Chronic Worry and Reclaim Your Life, Guilford, 2011

Pollack, Susan; Pedulla, Thomas; Siegel, Ronald; Sitting Together: Essential Skills for Mindfulness-Based Psychotherapy, Guilford, 2014

Santorelli, Saki, Heal Thyself: Lessons on Mindfulness in Medicine, Bell Tower, 1999

Sears, Richard, Building Competence in Mindfulness-Based Cognitive Therapy: Transcripts and Insights for Working With Stress, Routledge, 2015

Semple, Randye; Lee, Jennifer; <u>Mindfulness-Based Cognitive Therapy for Anxious Children: A Manual for Treating Childhood Anxiety</u>, New Harbinger, 2011

Siegel, Ronald, <u>The Mindfulness Solution: Everyday Practices for Everyday Problems</u>, Guilford, 2010

Siegel, Dan, <u>The Mindful Therapist: A Clinician's Guide to Mindsight and Neural Integration</u>, Norton, 2010

Stahl, Bob; Goldstein, Elisha; <u>A Mindfulness-Based Stress Reduction Workbook</u>, New Harbinger, 2010

Williams, Mark; Penman, Danny; <u>Mindfulness: An Eight-Week Plan for Finding Peace in a Frantic World</u>, Rodale Press, 2012

Wolf, Christiane; Serpa, Greg; <u>A Clinician's Guide to Teaching Mindfulness: The Comprehensive Session-by-Session Program for Mental Health Professionals and Health Care Providers</u>, New Harbinger, 2015

Link to Dropbox files

For a link to the guided meditations on Dropbox, type this into your URL line: LearnMindfulnessNYC.com/audio-link/ (Be sure to copy it exactly)

Or send an e-mail to info@DonaldFleck.com

Mindfulness events and teachings by Donald Fleck

Donald's web-site: LearnMindfulnessNYC.com

Donald's Announcements and mindfulness news:

Copy this line into your url: http://eepurl.com/buW3bj

www.ingramcontent.com/pod-product-compliance
Lightning Source LLC
Chambersburg PA
CBHW071029280326
41935CB00011B/1512